Economics of a Pure Gold Standard

Economics of a Pure Gold Standard

Mark Skousen

The Foundation for Economic Education, Inc.
Irvington-on-Hudson, New York

Economics of a Pure Gold Standard

Published by:

The Foundation for Economic Education, Inc.
30 South Broadway
Irvington-on-Hudson, NY 10533
(914)-591-7230

Publisher's Cataloging in Publication
(Prepared by Quality Books, Inc.)

Skousen, Mark.
Economics of a pure gold standard / by Mark Skousen. — 3rd. ed.

p. cm.
Includes biographical references and index
ISBN 1-57246-052-0

1. Gold standard. 2. Monetary policy. I. Title

HG297.S56 1996 332.4'222
QBI96-20302

Library of Congress Catalog Card Number: 96-85014

Cover design by Beth R. Bowlby
Manufactured in the United States of America

To Royal

Table of Contents

Acknowledgements

Several scholars have been helpful in the preparation of this work. I am especially thankful to the following people at George Washington University: Ching-Yao Hsieh, Professor of Economics; Joseph Aschheim, Professor of Economics; Peter Hill, Professor of History; John W. Kendrick, Professor of Economics; Henry Solomon, Dean of the Graduate School of Arts and Sciences; and Arthur E. Burns, Professor Emeritus of Economics.

I would also like to thank Murray N. Rothbard, Professor of Economics at the University of Nevada, Las Vegas, who stimulated my interest in this topic and offered several suggestions for research; also, Larry T. Wimmer, Professor of Economics at Brigham Young University, and Laurence S. Moss, Visiting Associate Professor of International Finance at The Fletcher School of Law and Diplomacy, Tufts University, for reading the manuscript and offering suggestions; and finally, to Arthur F. Burns and Milton Friedman for offering encouragement to me in this important study of monetary theory.

Preface to the Third Edition

In this third revised edition, I have added a significant section to chapter 4 examining the prospects of inflation, deflation and economic stability under a pure gold standard. In addition, in this new preface I address the major issues recently raised regarding gold: Did the gold standard cause the Great Depression? Should governments sell their precious metals? Is it possible to go back on a gold standard? Is the yellow metal a good indicator of inflationary expectations? Is free banking a superior monetary system?

A "pure" gold standard is defined as a monetary system wherein all monies, including banknotes and demand deposits, are backed one hundred percent by gold. This is quite distinct from a gold exchange standard, which is based on a fractional reserve banking system tied to a fixed price for gold. The gold exchange standard, which existed prior to 1971, proved to be unreliable and incapable of preventing monetary crises. But a 100 percent reserve commodity standard would be a vast improvement over the gold exchange standard. Based on both historical evidence and the unique properties of the yellow metal, I demonstrate that a pure gold standard provides a remarkably stable monetary system, far superior to the current precarious system based on discretionary central banking and fiat money. In fact, I conclude that a 100 percent gold standard closely approximates the ideal standard proposed by Milton Friedman and the monetarists. I offer two reasons.

Gold as an Ideal Standard

First, because of gold's indestructible nature, world monetary reserves and above-ground gold supplies are always rising (see figure 1, p. 84). Historically, they have never declined. Consequently, the monetarist goal of gradual growth in the money supply is achievable under gold.

Furthermore, under a 100 percent gold system, a monetary deflation, wherein the money supply declines, is virtually impossible. Thus, if the United States had operated on a 100 percent specie reserve system in the 1930s, the money stock could not have collapsed by a third and precipitated the Great Depression, as occurred under the Federal Reserve and a defective fractional-reserve banking system.

Second, monetary inflation is likely to be relatively low under gold, another desirable feature. Since 1492, the world's supply of yellow metal has never increased by more than five percent in any one year. Except for temporary gold rushes, the world's above-ground gold supplies have increased at a steady one-to-two percent per annum. World monetary reserves have risen at similar rates. While a gold-based system would not provide a mechanistic monetarist rule (where the money supply grows at a constant rate, say, four percent per year), it would be far less volatile than current monetary policies around the world.

Of course, individual nations may suffer occasional domestic periods of deflation or inflation, and the adjustment period following net imports or exports of precious metals may not be easy.[1] Historically, gold rushes have caused double-digit infla-

---

1. Jonathan E. Lewis argues that occasional domestic inflationary flare-ups and balance-of-payments problems could develop in major countries if the world returned to a gold standard. "In the countries attracting the gold, Britain and Germany, the stimulative monetary effect of the gold influx would disrupt both countries' attempts to control inflation." See his article, "Dream On, Gold Bugs," *The Wall Street Journal* (December 5, 1991, p. A15).

tion in some countries. Fortunately, gold-based supply shocks are not inherently cyclical. The subsequent rise in prices is not necessarily followed by a deflationary collapse, since the monetary stock rises but never declines. Prices are likely to remain at a higher plateau rather than drop precipitously after a gold rush.

A pure gold standard is not likely to support a stable price level, however. In fact, prices are likely to decline gradually over the long run if gold production does not match economic growth. Under the classic gold standard in England and the United States (1821–1914), the wholesale price index tended to be slightly deflationary (see figures 3a and 3b, pp. 110–11). A gently falling price level should not present any difficulties, however, as long as prices remain flexible and free from government control. At the same time, wage rates may not fall in the face of gently declining prices if worker productivity rises. Interest rates, reflecting the relative stable monetary growth pattern, are likely to remain low, thus providing a favorable climate for economic growth and long-term financing. (Under the classic gold standard, some long-term bonds matured in 100 years!)

Significantly, monetarists have recently begun to recognize the natural advantages of a genuine gold standard. Milton Friedman, in particular, has reversed his position that gold mining is an economic burden on society. He now acknowledges the argument, made originally by Professor Roger Garrison (Auburn), that the cost of mining and storing precious metals has not diminished since the world went off the gold standard. In a recent conversation, Friedman suggested that there were no longer any economic arguments against gold as an ideal monetary system, only political deterrents. That's a dramatic change from a generation ago when virtually all economists, including Ludwig von Mises and Joseph Schumpeter, felt that the gold standard could only be justified on political, not economic, grounds.

Did the Gold Standard Cause the Great Depression?

Anti-gold sentiment is still prevalent, however, among economists, journalists, and government officials. The latest assault comes from economists Barry Eichengreen (Berkeley) and Peter Temin (MIT), who argue that the international gold standard forced central bankers into precipitating the Great Depression of the 1930s. They conclude that a well-managed fiat-money system is superior to gold.[2]

Unfortunately, Eichengreen and Temin misinterpret history. They blame the gold standard for the 1929–33 debacle, but it was really a gradual movement away from the classical gold standard that precipitated the crisis. Eichengreen admits that the pre-1914 classical gold standard worked well, but broke down due to the inflationary policies of European powers during World War I.

The classical gold standard required issuers of money to hold sufficient gold reserves to handle the demands of individuals who wished to redeem their currencies into lawful money. National banknotes and bank reserves were redeemable in gold coins or bullion at any time. For example, each gold certificate issued by the U. S. Treasury contained the following declaration:

> **THIS CERTIFIES THAT THERE HAVE BEEN DEPOSITED IN THE TREASURY OF THE UNITED STATES OF AMERICA TWENTY DOLLARS IN GOLD COIN PAYABLE TO THE BEARER ON DEMAND.**

Although the U. S. Treasury did not maintain 100 percent specie reserves for all its legal obligations under the classical

2. See Barry Eichengreen, *Golden Fetters: The Gold Standard and the Great Depression, 1919-1939* (Oxford University Press, 1992), and Peter Temin, *Lessons from the Great Depression* (MIT Press, 1989). For a review of Eichengreen and Temin, see my column, "Did the Gold Standard Cause the Great Depression?", *The Freeman*, May 1995.

gold standard, it did hold more than 100 percent reserves to cover its gold certificates.

Eichengreen and other gold critics have pointed out that in a crucial time period, 1931–33, the Federal Reserve raised the discount rate for fear of a run on its gold deposits. If only the United States had not been on a gold standard, the critics say, the Fed could have avoided this reckless credit squeeze that pushed the country into depression and a banking crisis. However, the evidence contradicts this view. In fact, during the first two years of the contraction (1930–31), the U. S. gold stock rose! The Federal Reserve could have expanded its money supply during this critical time period. Instead, it reacted ineptly. As Milton Friedman and Anna Schwartz state, "We did not permit the inflow of gold to expand the U. S. money stock. We not only sterilized it, we went much further. Our money stock moved perversely, going down as the gold stock went up."[3] In short, even under the defective gold exchange standard, there was room to avoid a devastating worldwide depression and monetary crisis.

Should Governments Sell Their Gold?

Attacks on the gold standard have not just come from the Keynesians. Even some conservative economists have recommended that the United States sell off its gold stock. Recently Professor Richard Timberlake (University of Georgia) argued that since gold plays no current role in international monetary policy, the U.S. Treasury should sell its 260 million ounces of gold stock to the public.[4]

However, there is growing evidence that gold still plays an important, albeit limited, role in international affairs. Many central bankers monitor the price of gold as an important indi-

---

3. Milton Friedman and Anna J. Schwartz, *A Monetary History of the United States, 1867-1960* (Princeton University Press, 1963), pp. 360-61.

4. Richard Timberlake, "How Gold Could Be Money Again," *The Freeman*, April 1996.

cator of inflationary expectations and financial stability. Some economists (including Milton Friedman) have suggested that central bankers have attempted to peg the price of gold by buying or selling part of their gold holdings from time to time. Why? Because the world's governments do not want to see a massive inflation or deflation. For example, a rapidly rising gold price could destabilize the world's financial markets.

During the 1990s, some foreign governments sold some of their gold in an attempt to keep the price of gold from rising. Eventually, however, they will run out of gold to sell and prices will inevitably go higher. If the U.S. Treasury sells off its entire stock, as Professor Timberlake suggests, it could even cause a run on the dollar, the world's reserve currency, pushing gold prices sharply higher. Foreign currency traders might react negatively to the realization that the dollar is nothing more than paper.

In this regard, it is interesting to note that Switzerland, the country with the world's strongest currency, considers gold a vital asset. It is the only nation that by law must hold gold in reserve to cover its currency. At today's prices (approximately $400 an ounce), the value of its gold stock covers over 100 percent of its Swiss franc banknotes. The Swiss are not selling their gold.

If the U.S. monetary authorities wish to strengthen the dollar, they might consider following Switzerland's lead. What would it take to back all U.S. dollar banknotes with gold? Given the total U.S. currency of approximately $400 billion and a current gold stock of 260 million ounces, worth about $104 billion, there is a shortfall of $296 billion in uncovered banknotes. To make up the shortfall, the Treasury would have to buy approximately 740 million ounces of gold on the open market at a cost of $296 billion, assuming it could do so at the prevailing price ($400 an ounce).

After backing its banknotes, the United States could declare a gold standard, wherein each dollar bill is redeemable at a fixed amount of gold (based on the prevailing price of gold). The Treasury would be required to buy or sell gold at a fixed dollar amount. Thus, each banknote becomes a gold certificate, similar to those issued prior to 1933. Instead of saying "Federal Reserve Note," each hundred dollar bill would declare, "There have been deposited in the Treasury of the United States of America One Hundred Dollars in Gold Coin payable to the bearer on demand." This two-step policy would allow each citizen to redeem his share of government gold at any time, simply by presenting dollar bills at the Treasury window.

Once the government established a gold standard, commercial banks and other financial institutions could be granted the right to issue their own gold certificates, which could compete with government currency. They could also compete with the Treasury in minting gold coins (one ounce, half ounce, quarter ounce and tenth ounce), since gold coins would begin circulating along side gold certificates (dollar bills).

By establishing a fixed-exchange rate between gold and the dollar, gold coins and gold certificates could once again become popular mediums of exchange. Gold coins could once again circulate, as they did prior to 1933. If the United States pursued a gold standard, other nations would probably follow, thus establishing an international gold standard.

Granted, this gold-certificate program is not a complete 100 percent system, since demand deposits (checking accounts) are not covered. But I believe this gold-backed monetary standard would provide a much more stable environment than our current fiat-currency system.

Is Free Banking the Answer?

A growing number of free-market economists favor "free banking" as the ideal monetary standard. According to George Selgin, Larry White, and other free-bankers, a deregulated *laissez faire* banking system could maximize monetary freedom as well as provide a stable economic environment. Unlike a 100 percent reserve system, free banking would not require any reserve requirements whatsoever. Although a common base metal is preferred as a bank reserve, it is not essential. "There is no government control of the quantity of exchange media. There is no state-sponsored central bank. There are no legal barriers to the entry, branching, or exit of commercial banks. . . . There are no reserve restrictions. . . . There are no government deposit guarantees."[5]

However, there are still a great many concerns about free banking, especially with regard to potential systemwide bank runs and crises of confidence. With banks able to set reserve ratios as low as two percent, the potential for inflation and a subsequent destablizing boom-bust cycle seems high.[6] Selgin and White deny any problems as long as banks are permitted to adopt nationwide branch banking, contractual suspension clauses, and mutual-fund-based payment accounts, but other free-market economists fear that free banking provides far less confidence than a 100 percent program. But why adopt a monetary system that raises issues of confidence when the nation can embrace a monetary system that guarantees stability?

Gold as an Inflation Monitor

While the debate over the ideal monetary program continues, gold will remain a device for monitoring inflationary expectations and a hedge against economic uncertainty. Demand for the yellow metal is increasing around the world, especially in Asia, where people have a tradition of buying precious metals.

It is unfortunate that the establishment media still does not recognize gold as an accurate measure of economic, political, and military stability around the world. Neither *The New York Times* nor *The Wall Street Journal* highlight the price of

5. George A. Selgin and Lawrence H. White, "How Would the Invisible Hand Handle Money?", *Journal of Economic Literature,* December 1994, pp. 1718-49.

6. George Selgin, *The Theory of Free Banking* (Rowman & Littlefield, 1988), p. 140.

gold. *The Wall Street Journal*'s front-page summary of the markets announces indices for stocks, bonds, currencies, oil, and other commodities, but the yellow metal is deliberately omitted. I wrote the *Journal* a letter asking why and received a reply. "The editors don't agree with your claim that gold is the best indicator of inflationary expectations and economic stability," responded Dan Hinson, one of the *Journal*'s editors (correspondence, April 14, 1995).[7]

Is gold a good measure of inflationary expectations? Look at the chart below, which links the price of gold with the Consumer Price Index.

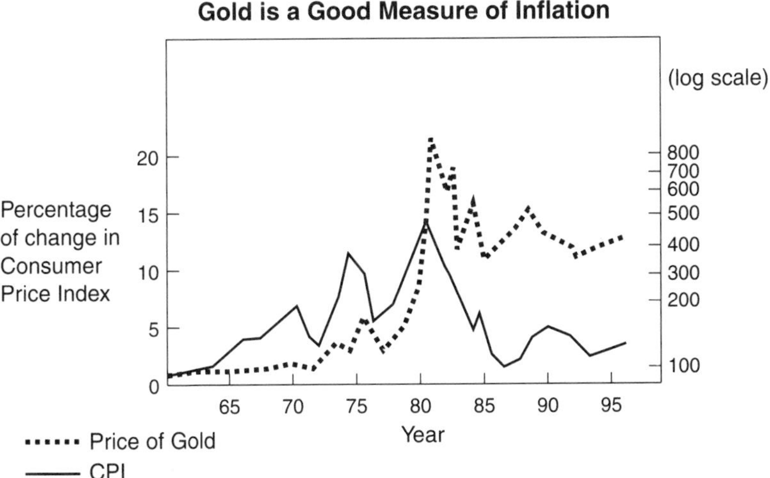

The fit is quite significant. When the world went off the gold exchange standard in 1971, the price of gold rose sharply from $35 an ounce to $200 an ounce, reflecting the sharp rise in commodity and consumer prices in 1973–74. Then gold suddenly topped out in 1975, about the same time the CPI rate starting dropping. When consumer price inflation started mov-

7. For a discussion of this and other gold-related issues, see *The Lustre of Gold* (Irvington-on-Hudson, N.Y.: The Foundation for Economic Education, 1995).

ing up again, reaching 14 percent in 1979–80, gold moved in sympathy, rising from $100 an ounce in 1976 to $850 an ounce in January, 1980. The long disinflationary era of the 1980s and 1990s saw a declining trend in both consumer price inflation and the gold price, although that trend may be changing again soon.

In short, it appears that the price of gold does a good job of reflecting the inflationary environment as measured by the Consumer Price Index. It is certainly a better indicator than the crude oil price. The editors of *The Wall Street Journal* and other establishment media need to rethink their anti-gold bias.

Gold isn't just another commodity. Gold is money. Some day an international monetary crisis may rudely awaken us to this reality.

Mark Skousen
January, 1996

Preface to the Second Edition (1988)

Support for returning to a gold standard is growing, not only among laymen but economists and politicians as well. There is an increasing uneasiness about the international fiat "dollar" standard and its apparent inability to provide stability in the foreign exchange markets, even in times of low inflation. Without some kind of independent monetary yardstick, the world's currencies seem to be at sea without a rudder.

In some ways we are already witnessing a return to gold, in terms of a "de facto gold standard." Central bankers are monitoring the free-market price of gold and using it as a barometer of international economic stability. There is evidence that some may even be using the gold price to determine the direction of monetary policy. If the price of gold rises, it indicates higher inflation and greater instability which could precipitate an economic or political crisis. If the price of gold declines, it suggests lower inflation and greater control over the world economy.

In addition, private investors around the world continue to hedge against an uncertain future by purchasing gold coins and storing them away. Citizens of the United States have joined the rest of the world in demanding gold-related investments. Gradually the U.S. government has shifted its former anti-gold stance toward pro-gold, legalizing gold ownership and gold-clause contracts, and finally, issuing legal tender U.S. gold coins in convenient sizes.

These monetary events have led me to revise and update my original doctoral thesis on "The 100 Percent Gold Standard:

Economics of a Pure Commodity Money." It used to be that the economic arguments in favor of gold took a back seat to the political case for gold. I wrote this book in order to raise the principal economic issues under various monetary constitutions, and to compare the gold standard with a fiat money standard.

The greatest challenge facing the hard-money movement is to figure out a practical way to reestablish a gold standard, and to determine what kind of gold standard may be adopted. Several free-market economists have attempted to do this, but it is still a delicate and difficult task.

I do not think that a gold standard will be reestablished on its own. No doubt such an event would *create* a crisis. But if a fiat dollar monetary crisis is already happening, a return to gold may actually reestablish economic stability.

1

Introduction

In Joseph A. Schumpeter's classic work, *History of Economic Analysis*, a careful distinction is made between "theoretical metallism" and "practical metallism." Theoretical metallism incorporates all *economic* arguments supporting the thesis that money requires the full backing of gold or silver. Practical metallism, on the other hand, justifies a specie money standard solely on the basis of *political*, or *non-economic*, reasons. Schumpeter elaborates: "An economist may, for instance, be fully convinced that theoretical metallism is untenable, and yet be a strong practical metallist. Lack of confidence in the authorities or politicians . . . is quite sufficient to motivate practical metallism in a theoretical cartelist [one who denies that money must be backed by a commodity such as gold or silver]."[1]

In a footnote, Schumpeter provides little justification or insight for his rejection of theoretical metallism. "I am taking for granted that theoretical metallism is untenable, i.e., that it is not true that, as a matter of pure logic, money essentially consists in, or must be backed by, a commodity or several commodities whose exchange value as commodities are the logical basis of their value as money. . . ."[2]

In a similar vein, Friedrich A. Hayek, whose earlier writings favored the gold standard, argues that "On purely economic

1. Joseph A. Schumpeter, *History of Economic Analysis* (New York: Oxford, 1954), p. 289.
2. Ibid., p. 289n.

grounds it must be said that there are hardly any arguments which can be advanced for, and many serious objections which can be raised against, the use of gold as the international money." Nevertheless, Hayek notes, there are compelling political reasons for a gold standard: ". . . while an international standard is [un]desirable on purely economic grounds, the choice of gold with all its undeniable defects is made necessary entirely by political considerations."[3]

Ludwig von Mises, highly sympathetic to the gold standard, concurs: "Gold is not an ideal basis for a monetary system," he states. "Like all human creations, the gold standard is not free from shortcomings; but in the existing circumstances there is no other way of emancipating the monetary system from the changing influences of party politics and government interference. . . . The excellence of the gold standard is to be seen in the fact that it renders the determination of the monetary unit's purchasing power independent of the policies of governments and political parties. Furthermore, it prevents rulers from eluding the financial and budgetary prerogatives of the representative assemblies."[4]

These statements by Schumpeter, Hayek, and Mises reflect the waning influence that the gold standard has had not only on the monetary policies of the Western world, but among professional economists as well. Present economic analysis of monetary policy emphasizes the workings of fiat currencies, floating exchange rates, and various schemes aimed at controlling the growth of the money supply. Gold is relegated to the international sphere where, by near unanimity among members of the International Monetary Fund, it is playing a moribund role. Even political support for gold, which Hayek and Mises speak of so fondly, has waned remarkably, despite the frequent claim that today's high rates of currency depreciation are largely politically motivated.

Historically, economic thought on the subject of monetary policy has slowly shifted from the economics of a commodity or

---

3. Friedrich A. Hayek, *Monetary Nationalism and International Stability* (New York: Longmans, Green, 1937), p. 74.

4. Ludwig von Mises, *The Theory of Money and Credit* (New Haven, Conn.: Yale University Press, 1953), p. 4.

specie standard to the economics of a fiduciary paper money standard. In the interim, academic economists and political leaders struggled with the issues of gold standard and convertibility, while the concept of 100 percent reserves was viewed as an unattainable, if not undesirable, goal. This trend was not necessarily intentional, but in large part was due to the fact that the historic gold standard, drifting from the gold bullion standard to the gold exchange standard, had fatal flaws that eventually contributed signally to its breakdown in 1933 and virtual abandonment in 1971.

The primary purpose of this work is not to detail the reasons why the historic gold standard finally collapsed, but modern critics primarily point to the ability of Western governments to expand their note and deposit obligations far in excess of their legal gold reserves, resulting eventually in the panic and depression which the fractional reserve gold standard was unable to prevent.[5]

As a result, the economic theory of a commodity standard, particularly of a pure commodity or uninhibited specie monetary policy, has been sorely neglected in recent decades. Over the centuries few economic and political thinkers have espoused such a "hard money" system, especially as the political climate and monetary policies have shifted further and further from a "pure" commodity standard. In this regard, Mises notes, "The gold standard lost popularity because for a very long time no serious attempts were made to demonstrate its merits and to explode the tenets of its adversaries."[6]

The 100 Percent Tradition

The foundations of a pure specie standard are highly idealistic and theoretical. However, such a monetary system did exist his-

---

5. For a revealing history of the quasi-gold standard and development of central banking, see Murray Rothbard, *The Mystery of Banking* (New York: Richardson & Snyder, 1983), pp. 179-254. See also, Ron Paul and Lewis Lehrman, *The Case for Gold* (Washington, D.C.: Cato Institute, 1982), pp. 17-142, and Michael D. Bordo, "The Gold Standard: Myths and Realities," in Barry N. Siegel, editor, *Money in Crisis* (San Francisco: Pacific Institute, 1984), pp. 208-226.

6. Mises, *Theory of Money and Credit*, p. 416.

torically. During the embryonic developments of money, the precious metals played a fundamental role, and for centuries, even up through the Middle Ages, survived without the introduction of fiduciary elements (though frequent aberrations occurred through the use of token coins). Economic theory had not advanced significantly during this ancient period of history, however. By the time the pre-classical and classical views of economic policy had unfolded in the 17th and 18th centuries, the introduction by the goldsmith-bankers of banknotes and credit instruments, far in excess of the precious metals they represented, had already taken place and become entrenched in Western economic society. As a result, from this time forward, the great majority of economists have been preoccupied with the theoretical implications of a fractional reserve system, rather than a 100 percent system. Though there have been several concentrated efforts to return to a pure specie standard, the Currency Principle and the Peel Act of 1844 being the most prominent, no Western government has approached this "hard money" principle. Concerning the Peel Act, John H. Williams comments: ". . . there has never been that 'automatic' working of the gold standard which the English Bank Act of 1844 was designed to insure."[7]

Despite the lack of historical precedent in modern times of a full-fledged commodity standard, a substantial literature on the subject has developed over the years. Judging from the writings of Schumpeter, Hayek and Mises, as quoted previously, it appears that the advocates of a 100 percent specie standard and their economic arguments have been largely overlooked or perhaps disregarded. The 100 percent monetary program, with its many tenets, has a long tradition in academic as well as economic history. During the embryonic developments of banking, the banks of Amsterdam, Hamburg, and Venice were 100 percent institutions and were referred to as "banks of deposit," and by statute were prohibited from lending out depositors' funds.

---

7. John H. Williams, "The Crisis of the Gold Standard," in Frederic C. Lane and Jelle C. Riemersma, eds., *Enterprise and Secular Change* (Homewood, Ill.: Irwin, 1953), p. 392.

Financial panics and foreign exchange crises during the 18th and early 19th centuries led to heavy resistance in America and England to the overissue of banknotes and "wild cat banking." During this time, founding fathers such as Thomas Jefferson, John Adams, John Quincy Adams, and Governor Thomas Randolph—and later the Jacksonians—popularized this "anti-banking" movement and all wrote in favor of either a pure 100 percent gold-money, or 100 percent gold backing for paper. The Currency School in England, led by George Norman, Samuel Jones Loyd, and Robert Torrens, adopted a similar stance by advocating that future issues of notes by the Bank of England be strictly backed by specie.

Following the Civil War in America, and the failure to incorporate deposits as well as notes into the Bank Act of 1844 in England, the idea of a 100 percent commodity standard virtually disappeared from view. The problems of circulating banknotes and greenbacks, the issue of free silver, and fractional reserve banking, which by this time had become a thoroughly entrenched institution in America, became the prime issues which preoccupied economists and politicians.

During this important paradigmatic transition, however, a few political and economic writers of the day still maintained the 100 percent doctrine, including General Amasa Walker, Boston merchant Charles H. Carroll, and an official of the United States Assay Office, Isaiah W. Sylvester. On the continent, German economists Philip Joseph Geyer and J. L. Tellkampt favored fully covered note issues, and criticized the issuance of unbacked notes as an "artificial" stimulus to business that could not last.

After the demise of the gold exchange standard in 1933, the theoretical underpinnings of a pure commodity standard were largely ignored. The only economist to advocate a 100 percent gold standard during this period was Elgin Groseclose. The 100 percent fiduciary standard proposed by Irving Fisher during the 1930's depression offered numerous similarities to a pure specie standard, but Fisher's proposal was based on a fundamental rejection of both gold and the fractional reserve banking system.[8]

---

8. See, for example, Irving Fisher, *The Instability of Gold* (New York: Alexander Hamilton Institute, 1912).

In the post-World War II period, several prominent economists expressed a remarkably strong sympathy with a pure commodity standard. Hayek, for example, wrote that such a program was a step "in the right direction," and even characterized 100 percent gold as a stable monetary system, escaping the effects of the business cycle. Eventually, however, he abandoned it in favor of a fiat standard based on a raw commodity index formula,[9] and later a "denationalized" standard of privately issued currencies.[10] Milton Friedman, in justifying government intervention in monetary and banking affairs, considers the operations of a pure commodity plan; and though he rejects such a program in the end on the grounds of exorbitant production costs and political infeasibility, he comments favorably and concludes that "if it were feasible, the advantages might be well worth the cost."[11] For reasons previously stated, however, he opts in favor of Fisher's plan of 100 percent reserves backed by Federal Reserve notes and deposits.

A resurgence of interest in the 100 percent specie standard has recently developed in the midst of monetary crises and foreign exchange upheavals in the Western world during the past decade, which have been accompanied by a relatively rapid rise in the free market price of gold and other precious metals. Some ultrametallist economic and financial observers have predicted that the present international dollar standard will eventually result in such high rates of currency debasement that a pure specie standard will, ipso facto, be reintroduced into the monetary system by market forces.

One of the strongest academic advocates favoring a strict 100 percent specie program has been Murray N. Rothbard, professor of economics at the University of Nevada, Las Vegas, who wrote in favor of a pure gold standard as early as 1962. Rothbard contends

---

9. Friedrich A. Hayek, *Individualism and Economic Order* (Chicago: University of Chicago Press, 1948), pp. 209-19.

10. Hayek, *The Denationalization of Money* (London: The Institute of Economic Affairs, 1976).

11. Milton Friedman, *A Program for Monetary Stability* (New York: Fordham University Press, 1960), p. 81, 7.

that it is the only monetary system that is "compatible with the fullest preservation of the rights of property . . . [and] . . . assures the end of inflation, and with it, the business cycle."[12] An integral part of Rothbard's thesis is the Austrian theory of the business cycle, which is interwoven throughout the works of the 100 percent advocates.[13]

Operations of a Pure Specie Standard

The economic framework of a pure specie program has been a major point of discussion among proponents. Essentially, the goal has been to establish a stable monetary system as consistent as possible with the free market and voluntary decisions of individuals. The role of government would be minimized, limited to the enforcement of contracts and financial obligations and the eradication of banking "fraud" and similar violations of public trust. There are, of course, points of difference on the role of government, specifically in regard to legal tender laws, private vs. public coinage, and banking regulations.

Under the pure specie framework, the monetary unit of account would depend entirely upon the voluntary choices of individuals. Generally, from an historical point of view, this meant the choice of gold, silver, copper, and certain alloys used to make coins more durable. Gold bullion has been the most popular choice for the *numeraire*, though most 100 percent advocates have favored a parallel standard, allowing fluctuation in the exchange prices between gold and silver, as opposed to a fixed exchange rate under bimetallism.

The principles of banking have been of utmost concern under the 100 percent rule. The specie thesis would not deny the advantages of a paper currency, nor the right of private bankers to issue their own note obligations (although some proponents such as

---

12. Murray N. Rothbard, *The Case for a 100 Percent Gold Dollar* (Washington, D.C.: Libertarian Press, 1974), p. 35. Originally appeared in Leland B. Yeager, ed., *In Search of a Monetary Constitution* (Cambridge: Harvard University Press, 1962).

13. For a recent debate on the merits of various monetary systems based on gold, see *The Cato Journal*, Spring 1983 (Volume 3, No. 1).

Thomas Jefferson at times opposed notes altogether). Banknotes, however, are to be fully backed by the commodity-money and demand deposits are to be nothing more than warehouse receipts. The hard money adherents have been highly critical of the original goldsmith-bankers who discounted bills beyond their deposit holdings and lent out "demand deposits." This practice has been regarded by many as outright fraud and would be prohibited by law under the 100 percent rule. The question of fraud is of major importance, and a great deal of literature is devoted to this single issue. Advocates of a pure specie program have been highly critical of modern banking practices which mix the loan and deposit functions. Under a pure specie standard, these two functions would be strictly separated. Banks could, however, participate in lending activities as financial intermediaries and by other specified avenues.

Advocates of the 100 percent specie plan reject in general the concept of "free banking," which permits the issue of banknotes beyond specie as long as convertibility is upheld, as an ideal monetary system. As a practical decision, however, "free banking" has often been considered a "second best" solution to monetary ills, and though still regarded as a fraudulent practice, would provide a sounder monetary environment than would a central bank.

Economic Issues and Monetary Policy

The 100 percent specie standard would have complete automaticity and freedom from government control. According to its adherents, it would virtually eliminate international monetary crises and domestic runs on banks. It would force government to restrict its financing of expenditures to either taxation or borrowing, without the power of money creation. Proponents believe that the general price level would be far more stable under this kind of monetary system than under a fiat currency system. Moreover, it would eliminate the "inherent bankruptcy" of banking institutions, in which deposit liabilities are in short-term obligations while assets are in long-term investments.

On the other hand, critics maintain that the pure specie standard has a number of fatal flaws, including the high burden of production costs and an inelasticity of supply (which is considered, ironically, one of its major advantages by proponents). In this regard, it is worth noting a comparison between the 100 percent *commodity* standard versus the 100 percent *fiat paper* standard of money, as viewed as an ideal monetary system. There are both significant similarities and differences between the two plans. The debate centers around the questions of stability, inflation, costs, controlling the price level, and matters of philosophy as well.

In searching for an ideal monetary standard, it appears that, until recently, the virtues of paper money over specie, in terms of both costs and ability to control the stock of money, seemed overwhelming from an economic point of view. Now, however, several Austrian economists have made an important new challenge to the fiat paper standard from a purely economic point of view. Using a revitalized Mises-Hayek theory of the business cycle, they dispute the economic benevolence of a fiduciary currency over a commodity money. In essence, they charge that fiat money unbacked by fully embodied specie disrupts society's consumption/investment patterns, disorients aggregate supply and demand, and creates a business cycle. But, in contrast, because of certain elements peculiar to commodity money, a 100 percent specie standard eliminates these cyclical effects, though "fluctuations" do occur.

Contribution of the Hard Money School

At a time when Western governments are reexamining their international and domestic monetary policies and while the debate on the viability of a commodity standard ensues, a history of economic thought on the pure specie standard provides significant insights. Until now, no systematic study has been made of the history and contributions of the 100 percent hard money school. This presentation seeks to fill this important gap in the history of economic thought.

Despite the fact that this commodity money plan is highly theoretical and has not been instituted on a practical basis in modern history (though some valiant attempts have been made), the

100 percent advocates have made numerous important contributions to economic science and political economy. Highlights include the following ideas.

First, 100 percent supporters have consistently raised the ethical and legal deficiencies of fractional reserve banking, particularly with regard to the customer-banker relationship. Banking authorities, for example, have failed to come to grips with a problem which persists even to this day, i.e., the popular misconception that funds left on deposit with a bank are legally *owned* by the bank's customers. In reality, ownership is maintained by the bank, which becomes a debtor, while the customer becomes a creditor.

Second, the 100 percent group was the first to recognize the importance of demand deposits over banknotes in forming the largest portion of the stock of money (the British Currency School being a notable exception). They also offered significant theoretical implications on how changes in demand deposits affected loan demand, the money supply, and economic growth and stability (and vice versa).

Third, the idealistic hard money proponents have highlighted the harmful effects of excessive credit expansion through fractional reserve banking and inconvertible notes, and how credit expansion created cyclical patterns of boom and bust.

Fourth, gold advocates emphasize the central role of the free-market price of gold as a barometer of economic and monetary stability in the world.

By adopting an uncompromising, pure system of monetary theory, advocates of the 100 percent specie rule have emphasized the unstable nature of fractional reserve banking and areas where the banking system may contribute to cyclical patterns of economic activity. These are flaws in the banking system and monetary policy that may have gone unnoticed and uncorrected otherwise.

2

The 100 Percent Specie Tradition

The Origin of Money

Originally, money consisted entirely of fully-embodied commodities which had specific qualities suitable for a medium of exchange. In the early history of money, animal skins, sheep and cattle, slaves, jewelry, beads, shells, whales' teeth, engraved stones, tusks of ivory, grains, olive oil, cocoa nuts, tobacco, sugar, alcoholic beverages, and manufactured goods were used in various civilizations.[1]

As civilization developed, the metals—particularly iron, copper, silver, and gold—were discovered and their superior qualities as a medium of exchange became readily apparent. These qualities included portability, indestructibility, homogeneity, divisibility, cognizability, and relative stability of value compared with other commodities. As Jevons comments, "Some of the metals seem to be marked out by nature as most fit of all substances for employment as money, at least when acting as a medium of exchange and a store of value."[2]

The use of these metals as money took various forms. Ingots, stamped on one side only, served initially as coins and circulated by weight. The oldest specimens appear to have been privately minted by merchants, money changers, and miners. It was not

1. W. S. Jevons, "Early History of Money," *Money and the Mechanism of Exchange* (London: Kegan Paul, 1905), pp. 19-28. See also Carl Menger, *Principles of Economics*, edited by James Dingwall and Bert F. Hoselitz (Glencoe, Ill.: Free Press, 1950), pp. 263-67.

2. Jevons, *Money and Mechanism*, p. 40.

until about the 7th century B.C. that the first gold and silver coins were introduced in ancient Lydia.[3]

Thus, the pure specie tradition had a natural beginning in the marketplace, gradually growing out of the voluntary transactions of ancient peoples. In this context, Arthur Kemp notes, "History tells us quite clearly that money originated not in the actions of government but from the voluntary actions of merchants to facilitate their commerical exchanges, to promote preservation of purchasing power, and to aid in the formation of capital."[4] And Carl Menger comments, "The origin of money . . . is . . . entirely natural. . . . Money is not an invention of the state. It is not the product of a legislative act. Even the sanction of political authority is not necessary for its existence. Certain commodities came to be money quite naturally, as the result of economic relationships that were independent of the power of the state."[5]

Historically, however, the issue of money was seldom left to the market, and this was even apparent during the embryonic developments of money. Private coinage was crudely produced, and clipping and counterfeiting were widespread practices. In Greece, the government certified fineness in silver for the first time. State-issued and private coins existed side by side for centuries. Nevertheless, "The period of dependence upon private coining seems, in view of the scarcity of specimens of coins of private issues, to have been short. . . ."[6] Governments eventually began to certify both the fineness and weight of coins. However, losses due to wear did not necessarily result in a significant deviation from a full metallic

3. Arthur R. Burns, *Money and Monetary Policy in Early Times* (New York: Knopf, 1927), pp. 59-78. Cf. William Ridgeway, *The Origin of Metallic Currency and Weight Standards* (Cambridge, Mass.: Wilson, 1892), p. 205.

4. Arthur Kemp, "The Gold Standard: A Reappraisal," in Yeager, *In Search of a Monetary Constitution*, pp. 139-40.

5. C. Menger, *Principles*, pp. 261-62. Also: "As *each* economizing individual becomes increasingly more aware of his economic interest, he is led by this *interest, without any agreement, without legislative compulsion, and even without regard to the public interest*, to give his commodities in exchange for other, more saleable, commodities, even if he does not need them for any immediate consumption purpose" (p. 260).

6. Arthur R. Burns, *Money and Monetary Policy*, p. 78.

standard of money, and when measurable discrepancies occurred between actual and stipulated weight of the coins, coins gradually circulated by actual weight.[7]

Introduction of Token Coins

The 100 percent metallic standard was maintained while money circulated by tale as well as weight. Token bronze coins were first introduced in the last century B.C. in Rome, but "practically the only token coins in early times were small change money. Tokens tempted the counterfeiter, and the greater the difference between legal value and metallic value the greater the temptation."[8] As a result, principal coins were nearly always full-weight money, and the 100 percent monetary system was for all practical purposes preserved.

The issuance of token coins, a forerunner of paper money and banknotes, became a popular practice by governments throughout the Middle Ages. Governments recognized the problems of wear and tear of full-weight coins and substituted subsidiary brass or copper coins for purposes of trade and small transactions. There were more deceptive reasons as well, however. The history of coinage, from Rome to London, has been fraught with abuse. In numerous cases, gold and silver coins were certified by government decree equal to a specified fineness and weight, but then gradually the coins were debased by the government mint for political reasons. Amounts of metal were removed from the coins so that the market value of the coin was less than the legal value set by law—in essence, creating a token coin. Commenting on this era, Jevons writes, "The annals of coinage, in this and all other countries, are little more than a monotonous repetition of depreciated issues both public and private, varied by occasional meritorious, but often unsuccessful, efforts to restore the standard of the currency."[9]

---

7. W. S. Jevons, *Money and Mechanism*, p. 94: "But so soon as coins bear evidence of wear or ill-treatment, they must be circulated by weight. . . ."

8. Arthur R. Burns, *Money and Monetary Policy*, p. 313.

9. W. S. Jevons, p. 79.

Originally, the national currencies—the British pound, the German mark, the French franc, for example—were simply certain weights of either gold or silver bullion, and this formed the basis of a pure metallic monetary standard. "The English pound was once an actual pound of silver. . . ."[10] Later, however, due to coin debasing, the pound and other currencies no longer represented a weight of bullion, though the public still adhered to the pound and other national currencies as a unit of account or numeraire. To the extent that the public accepted legal tender coins on the basis of weight only rather than by tale, a pure metallic standard of money was preserved, and contemporary economic thinkers who favored full-weight coin were essentially proponents of a 100 percent specie standard. Fundamentally, the Western world during the Middle Ages operated under a specie standard, however tarnished over the years. Most significantly, the widespread introduction of token coins, which did not represent claims to full-weight coins, presented the first deviation from a full specie currency.

The Origin of Banking

The widespread debasement of currencies and the issuance of numerous kinds of token coins led to the development of banking in Italy. During the Middle Ages, 1400-1500 A.D., in Italy, ". . . the circulating medium consisted of a mixture of coins of many denominations, variously clipped or depreciated. In receiving money, the merchant had to weigh and estimate the fineness of each coin, and much trouble, loss of time, and risk of fraud thus arose. It became, therefore, the custom in the mercantile repub-

10. Francis A. Walker, *Money* (New York: H. Holt, 1891), p. 187. Jevons, *Money and Mechanism*, p. 87: The English pound sterling came from the "Saxon pound of standard silver." Also, Luigi Einaudi points out that the "pound sterling" was an "imaginary money" because the pound was never coined. However, the pound did originate from a pound of silver, and there really existed originally (at the time of Charlemagne) minted silver coins which totaled a pound weight. According to the translator's footnote, during Charlemagne's reign, "Two hundred and forty of such [silver] penies were cut from a pound weight" (Luigi Einaudi, "The Theory of Imaginary Money from Charlemagne to the French Revolution," in Lane and Riemersma, *Enterprise and Secular Change*, pp. 229-30).

lics of Italy to deposit such money in a bank, where its value was accurately estimated, once for all, and placed to the credit of the depositor."[11] These credits were called "bank-money" and they "commanded an *agio* or premium corresponding to the average depreciation of the coins. . . . The money paid was thus always of full value, and all trouble in counting and valuing was avoided."[12] The Bank of Venice, established in 1171, was essentially a "bank of deposits," where coins were weighed and assayed, and then credited by weight ("bank-money") to the account of the depositor.[13]

The development of banking in the Middle Ages, particularly in Italy, was based on the legal principles of Roman law. Private banking in Italy flourished as banks accepted deposits and lent out funds. According to Abbot Payson Usher, fractional reserves were frequently maintained, and "There was no period in which it would not have been lawful for a money changer to accept a deposit of funds which he might employ in trade or lend to others, subject only to the obligation to repay the depositor on demand in coin of equivalent value."[14]

Italian bankers (and later European bankers) offered two forms of deposits: First, general deposits—demand deposits, which were frequently lent out by deposit banks. Second, conditional deposits—consisting of:

> Actual deposits of specie to be paid to a designated party at a fixed date or after the performance of some definite act. . . . Funds to be paid on the transfer of property, sums to be paid over on dowries or marriage settlements, sums due in settlement of judgments in courts, the price of merchandise to be delivered at a later date, might all give rise to conditional deposits. The payor

---

11. W. S. Jevons, *Money and Mechanism*, p. 195.

12. Ibid., p. 196.

13. Amasa Walker, *Nature and Uses of Money and Mixed Currency* (Boston: Crosly, Nichols & Co., 1857), p. 20.

14. Abbot Payson Usher, "The Origin of Banking: The Primitive Bank of Deposit, 1200-1600," in Lane and Riemersma, eds., *Enterprise and Secular Change*, pp. 165-66.

placed the funds in the hands of the banker with an explicit understanding that they would be transferred to the payee when the conditions of their agreement had been fulfilled. Such funds did not constitute a part of the ordinary current account of either party. The payor was obviously barred from diverting such funds to other uses, and the payee could not use them because they did not become his property until the final transfer was made. In their primitive form, conditional deposits did not lead to any use of credit, but small changes made them useful in an important type of credit transaction.[15]

Continental Banks of Deposit

The unrestrained banking practices of the private Italian banks often led to reckless credit arrangements, bankruptcies and loss of funds, and consequently, local governments tried to impose more stringent restrictions on banking in Italy and in other European countries. In the early 17th century, the Giro banks were established in Venice, Genoa, and other Italian cities. They replaced the permissive private banks, at least temporarily, and "were hardly more than institutions for centralized clearance; actual credit operations were prohibited."[16]

In Germany, the Bank of Hamburg was established to weigh and assay all coins, which were then credited to the account of the depositor. A small commission was required of each depositor.[17] According to Amasa Walker, the bank "never promises more coin that it has in its vaults." Moreover, "It has never deranged trade by contraction or expansion. It has always been found reliable. It has contributed greatly to the prosperity of the city, and the convenience of all connected with Hamburg in trade."[18]

---

15. Ibid., p. 277. For example, the banker might allow the customer to overdraw his current account on the security of his credit.
16. Ibid., p. 290.
17. Amasa Walker, *Money and Mixed Currency*, p. 20.
18. Amasa Walker, *The Science of Wealth* (Boston: Little, Brown & Co., 1874), pp. 224-32; 226.

The Bank of Amsterdam was the most famous of the "banks of deposit." Adam Smith, in *The Wealth of Nations*, highlights the workings of the Amsterdam bank. "The bank of Amsterdam professes to lend out no part of what is deposited with it, but, for every guilder for which it gives credit in its books, to keep in its repositories the value of a guilder either in money or bullion."[19] Full 100 percent reserves were not maintained on its capital stock, however.

The Bank of Amsterdam was created by the Dutch government in 1609. Any citizen could make deposits and withdraw coin or bullion. A commission was charged equal to 1/40th of 1 percent on deposits and withdrawals. Other charges were exorbitant, more than required to maintain the bank's solvency, but were used to raise revenues for the government. Despite these high fees, the bank was very profitable. The bank's founders insisted on a strict separation of the lending and deposit functions of the bank. "It is clear that the original theory of the bank as a bank of deposit did not contemplate lending as one of its functions. Established without capital, it was understood, both by the ordinance which created it and by the public, to have actually in its vaults the whole amount of specie for which bank money was at any time outstanding."[20] Unfortunately, the bank did not live up to its charter. No public records were kept by the bank, and it was later discovered that the bank had surreptitiously lent 9 million guilder to the city of Amsterdam. As a result of public disclosures, the bank failed in 1791, after 182 years of existence.[21]

Concerning the continental banks of deposit in the 17th century, J. E. Thorold Rogers notes that the "bank-money" was "of the nature of dock warrants, entitling the holder to claim not only

---

19. Adam Smith, *An Inquiry into the Nature and Causes of the Wealth of Nations* (New York: The Modern Library, [1776] 1937), p. 453.

20. Charles F. Dunbar, *Chapters on the Theory and History of Banking* (New York: Putnam, 1901), p. 103. Adam Smith comments on other fees charged by the Bank of Amsterdam. See *The Wealth of Nations*, pp. 448-49.

21. Irving Fisher, *100% Money* (New Haven, Conn.: The City Printing Co., 1945), pp. 35-36. Dunbar, *Theory and History of Banking*, pp. 114-17.

the sum which they expressed, but, theoretically at least, the very coins which were deposited against them."[22]

Banking in England

Commercial deposit banking developed in the 17th century in England. Contrary to popular opinion, the goldsmiths were not the first English bankers. R. D. Richards, in his important work, *Early History of Banking in England*, provides evidence that "the money scrivener was a custodian of deposits before the goldsmith, and that the goldsmith was a dealer in bills of exchange before he became a recognized deposit keeper."[23]

Scriveners were clerks who had stewardship over their employers' accounts, and did not engage in fiduciary issue or fractional reserve banking. Primarily, they were the keepers of people's funds, and acted as trustees or custodians.

> During the sixteenth and early seventeenth centuries most of the book-keeping of the merchants was done by professional scriveners, who acted as cashiers for one or more merchants, kept their coffers, brought in their receipts, made their payments, and rendered them strict account of every transaction. The scrivener was an agent. His principal's money was not lent to him, but was merely in his charge. In a similar manner from early times the great landowners had employed a steward or cofferer, whose business it was to keep the household accounts and have charge of the treasure-chest.[24]

In addition, "The scriveners were small men with little capital and of no great repute in the City; but they were agents, bound to

---

22. J. E. Thorold Rogers, *First Nine Years of the Bank of England* (London, 1887), p. 8.

23. R. D. Richards, *Early History of Banking in England* (London: P. S. King & Sons, 1929), p. 227.

24. A. E. Feaveryear, *The Pound Sterling* (Oxford: Marendon Press, 1963), p. 92. Cf. Richards, *Early Banking in England*, p. 223.

keep their employers' money safely, and criminally liable if they used it for their own purposes."[25]

The Role of the Goldsmiths

The financial position of the goldsmiths was in sharp contrast with that of the scriveners. Goldsmiths were generally merchants and aldermen who had capital of their own and lent money to kings (such as to King Edward III) and to other merchants. These advances "were made out of their profits as craftsmen, jewelers and bullion merchants."[26]

Landowners and merchants gradually transferred funds from stewards and scriveners to the goldsmiths, especially during the Civil War and Commonwealth period of English history, for fear of the safety of their treasure. In addition, "English merchants had been in the custom of depositing their cash in the London Tower, until Charles I seized £120,000 of the treasure in 1640, and repaid it only after long delay and much protest. As a result, merchants and nobles began to leave their coin and valuables with the goldsmiths, receiving in exchange the goldsmiths' receipts or notes."[27]

It is clear that, at first, the goldsmiths acted as trustees for the funds they received. It involved the

> accepting of money deposits in trust, the custody of money which the custodian was not allowed to use. Money thus deposited was, for a small payment, kept in chests or sealed in bags, and was returned on demand, while the receipts given were simply warehouse dockets. The goldsmith was the trustee or bailee, and the depositor the bailor. The records of the Goldsmith's Company of London show that a number of metropolitan goldsmiths functioned as bailees of valuables and of money during the reign of James I and Charles I. . . . The first notes issued by the goldsmiths were, as we have seen, bailee notes, or non-assignable warehouse receipts.[28]

---

25. Ibid., p. 95.
26. R. D. Richards, *Early Banking in England*, p. 223.
27. Elgin Groseclose, *Money and Man* (New York: Frederick Ungar, 1961), pp. 177-78. See also Jevons, *Money and Mechanism*, pp. 196-97.
28. R. D. Richards, *Early Banking in England*, pp. 223, 225.

Ellis T. Powell, in *The Evolution of the Money Markets*, reports that "originally the goldsmith's customers were unaware of the profit which he made by the use of the money. They deposited it only for safekeeping, with one who held himself out as a gratuitous bailee. The goldsmith made himself into a kind of safe deposit, accepting the custody of gold and silver plate, ornaments, metal, and specie, including foreign coins of varied origin and denomination."[29]

Obviously, the depositing of bullion and coins with goldsmiths and the issuing of notes or receipts for these deposits, which circulated as money, did not alter the pure metallic standard. As long as the receipts were bonafide and backed by an equal amount of metal on deposit, the 100 percent standard was maintained in an efficient manner.

The character of the goldsmith qua banker changed gradually, undoubtedly as a result of the financial-lending functions the goldsmiths primarly engaged in prior to becoming trustees of people's funds. They were simply never attuned to serve as bailees of customers' valuables. Originally, they were lenders and middlemen, established as financial intermediaries, and ". . . money was lent to them as principals, and if they employed it for their own ends and lost it, there was only a civil remedy."[30]

How did fractional reserve banking come about? First, regarding goldsmith notes, "Because it represented the actual deposit of money, it came to be freely received in private transactions as money. Though the goldsmith's note was never tender, it served to accustom the commercial community with the use of paper equivalents of money."[31]

Gradually, the goldsmiths "noticed the influence of the 'law of great numbers' on their increasing volume of business: their deposits and withdrawals largely offset each other."[32] Consequently,

---

29. Ellis T. Powell, *The Evolution of the Money Markets* (London: Cass, 1966), p. 62. His report is based on the tract, "The Mystery of the New-Fashioned Goldsmith," incorporated in J. B. Martin, *Grasshopper in Lombard Street* (1676).

30. A. E. Feaveryear, *Pound Sterling*, p. 95.

31. Elgin Groseclose, *Money and Man*, p. 178.

32. Wilhem Röpke, *Economics of a Free Society* (Chicago: Regnery, 1963), p. 89.

the goldsmith-bankers were able to issue notes in excess of the amount of specie held on deposit. On a critical note, Groseclose observes, "It was only a step to the discovery by the more unprincipled goldsmiths that funds of clients might be lent out so long as the goldsmith retained on hand sufficient amounts to meet anticipated calls for the return of deposits."[33]

Thus, the transformation into fractional reserve banking occurred through the peculiar nature of the goldsmith receipts, which began to be transferred as representative money: ". . . at first these documents were special promises, like dock warrants. The practice arose of transferring possession by delivery of these receipts, or 'goldsmith's notes,' as they were called. Such notes are frequently referred to in Acts of Parliament, and even as late as 1746 most of the London bankers continued to be members of the Goldsmith's Company. It is plain from the manner in which these notes were mentioned in some statutes that they had become general and not special promises—merely engagements to deliver a sum of money on demand, without conditions as to keeping a reserve for the purpose."[34]

Because of the background and training of the goldsmiths as money lenders, the use of depositors' funds appeared almost natural to them as long as sufficient funds were held in reserve to meet depositors' demands. Thus, the relationship between the customer and the banker gradually changed from a bailor-bailee to a creditor-debtor relationship. "Thus the goldsmith bailee developed into the debtor of the depositor; and the depositor became an investor who loaned his money to the goldsmith for a 'consideration.' "[35] Instead of warehouse receipts, the goldsmith's notes became promissory notes representing an amount of cash withdrawable on call, and these notes were payable to a specified person or to bearer.

---

33. E. Groseclose, p. 178. R. G. Hawtrey accuses the goldsmiths as "they who made an illicit profit by 'clipping' the silver coins, or sorting out the heavy coins for export or melting." Idem., *Currency and Credit* (London: Longmans, Green & Co., 1919), p. 289.

34. W. S. Jevons, *Money and Mechanism*, p. 197.

35. R. D. Richards, *Early Banking in England*, p. 223.

This gradual change was not obvious to the depositor, who still regarded the "deposit" as his own property, and not lent to the banker. Powell outlines this transformation of the legal relationship between the banker and his customers: "We saw him [goldsmith-banker], originally, as a bailee. But the bailee is precluded from using the bailed chattel for his own personal advantage, in any manner whatsoever, without the express consent of the bailor, unless such use be needful for its preservation (as in the giving of exercise to a bailed horse)."[36] Powell points out that, according to the legal codes concerning the bailee-bailor relationship, the bailee was required to return the "identical thing deposited, which would border upon the impossible in the case of coined money. . . . Money had no Earmark. One penny cannot be known from another."[37]

Thus, the fungibility of money, coupled with the nature of business the goldsmiths were accustomed to, permitted a drastic change in banking—from the legal status of bailee to that of debtor. How this legal change was made is raised by Powell:

> When, then, did it begin to be the accepted doctrine that the banker was merely the debtor, and not the bailee, much less the trustee, of his customer? What circumstances led to this modification of his legal position and produced an economic "sport" which has changed the whole outlook of finance and added incalculably to its power? How did the note or receipt become disconnected from the *specific* deposit, and available only against the banker generally?[38]

The change was an evolutionary one. During the 17th and 18th centuries, bank customers filed suit over fractional reserve banking and the legal status of customers' deposits. In nearly every case, the courts ruled consistently that the banker was only a debtor and not a bailee or trustee. Why? Principally because the money or coins in storage were not specifically identifiable. This

---

36. E. T. Powell, *Evolution of Money Markets*, pp. 63-64.
37. Ibid., p. 64.
38. Ibid.

was the *sine qua non* in any case involving theft or robbery of property—the stolen property or goods must, according to the courts, be identifiable. But individual customers' coins could not be identified. Thus, because of the fungible nature of money, the banker could not be held accountable as a bailee. The courts treated the banking situation just as they would any other case dealing with fraud or theft; they simply did not see the special nature of money deposits; thus, "the bailment of money, in the shape of loose and therefore unidentifiable coins, where the bailor's only action for the recovery of the money is one of debt."[39]

The issue was not laid to rest in England until the early 19th century. Again, some depositors challenged the traditional rulings of the English courts, arguing that "banks should be held to a degree of responsibility little or nothing short of that which belongs to the class of bailees under which common carriers, innkeepers, and others are ranked."[40] However, "The court, in Pitts vs. Glegg, laid it down, in 1833, that sums which are paid to the credit of a customer with a banker, though usually called deposits, are in truth loans by the customer to the banker."[41] The courts did feel, however, that the use of the term "deposit" was misleading, though they still permitted its use by bankers. Elaborating on this view, Lord Cottenham in 1848, in the case of Foley vs. Hill, said,

> The money placed in the custody of a banker is, to all intents and purposes, the money of the banker, to do with it as he pleases; he is guilty of no breach of trust in employing it; he is not answerable to the principal if he puts it into jeopardy, if he engages in a hazardous speculation; he is not bound to keep it or deal with it as the property of his principal; but he is, of course, answerable for the amount, because he has contracted, having received that money, to repay to the principal, when demanded, a sum equivalent to that paid into his hands.[42]

39. Ibid., p. 68.
40. Ibid., p. 72.
41. Ibid., p. 73.
42. Ibid., p. 73n.

Therefore, in conclusion, Powell states, "The relationship between banker and customer as that of debtor and creditor, and not trustee and *cestui que trust*, or bailee and bailor, seems to have been regarded as an established fact—obvious, notorious, and practically unchallengable."[43]

Contemporary Views of Modern Banking

The change in the legal status of the banker opened the doors to legitimizing fractional reserve banking, which soon became a hallowed institution in Western society. No longer was it a question of the legal status of the banker-customer relationship, or whether banks should hold an amount of specie equal to depositors' claims. But rather the practical question became one of sound vs. unsound banking practices, and how much reserves should be maintained in order to preserve public trust. The terms "redeemability" and "claims of ownership" no longer applied; the watchwords became "convertibility" and the optimal "level of reserves." Moreover, under a fractional reserve system, "The essential practice of modern banking is that of maintaining obligations payable on demand, or on short notice, while holding 'cash' amounting to only a *small fraction* of these obligations."[44]

Once the legalization of fractional reserve banking was established, the question among reformers became: Is there an equilibrium level and reserve ratio which all banks would voluntarily tend to approach while still maintaining integrity and public confidence? Would "free banking," void of government regulations over the level of reserves as well as over branching, create a stable monetary climate? Or was government necessary to restrain banks from unduly depressing this reserve ratio to the point of creating an "infinite" supply of money, causing self-destruction and panic? Over the next couple of centuries, political and economic thinkers sought the answers to these questions.

---

43. Ibid., p. 71.

44. Henry C. Simons, *Economic Policy for a Free Society* (Chicago: University of Chicago Press, 1948), p. 319n.

Some critics were strongly influenced by history. The massive expansion of banknotes, bills of exchange, checks, and other forms of payment created an ubiquitous "anti-bank" sentiment during the 18th and 19th centuries. In England, political and economic philosopher David Hume was in the forefront over monetary matters and took a hard money stance, charging that bank credit expansion caused a rise in domestic prices, and this in turn put England at a disadvantage in foreign trade. Hume blamed fractional reserve banking for credit crises, foreign exchange losses and an outflow of specie. He considered the most desirable bank as one which locked up all the money and participated in no lending activities whatsoever. In essence, he supported the 100 percent system.[45]

American Reaction to Paper Money

In America, the colonists found themselves practically inundated with various forms of state-issued paper money, and at the same time were faced with the disastrous funding of the American revolutionary war with inconvertible Continentals. During the framing of the Constitution, sentiment was so strong against state-issued paper that a large majority of the delegates voted in favor of prohibiting outright this power to the states. One of the delegates at the convention reported, "As it was reported by the committee in detail, the States were only prohibited from emitting them without the consent of Congress; but the convention was so smitten with the paper money dread, that they insisted that the prohibition be absolute."[46] Advocates of this stronger action of prohibition included James Madison, Gouverneur Morris, Robert Morris, and George Mason. The language of the U.S. Constitution finally read: "No state shall . . . coin money, emit bills of credit; and make any thing but gold and silver coin a tender in payment of debts" (Article I, Section 10).

---

45. David Hume, *Political Discourses* (1752), pp. 43-45, 89-91. Cf. Hume, *Banks and Paper Money, Financial Pamphlet*, v. 22. Hume had influence on two contemporary reformers, Patrick Murray Elibank, *Essays* (1755), pp. 20-25, and Joseph Harris, *An Essay Upon Money and Coins* (1757-58), Part I, pp. 100-102.

46. Max Farrand, ed., *The Records of the Federal Convention of 1787* (New Haven, 1937), Vol. III, p. 214.

The Constitutional Convention also debated the question whether the federal government should have the power to emit bills of credit, which were technically short-term borrowing instruments, but often became legal tender currency. This, then, raised the real issue of the issuance of paper money by the federal government. Many of the "hard money" advocates, who previously favored the prohibition of issuing paper money by state legislatures, refused to support a motion to prohibit a similar issue by the federal congress. Concerning George Mason, for example, "Though he had a mortal hatred of paper money, yet as he could not foresee all emergencies, he was unwilling to tie the hands of the Legislature."[47]

Nevertheless, the convention voted against the motion to permit the government to "emit bills of credit." By doing so, James Madison "became satisfied that striking out the words would not disable the Government from the use of public notes, as far as they could be safe and proper; and would only cut off the pretext for a paper-currency and particularly for making the bills a tender either for public or private debts."[48]

Commenting on the convention, Albert Gallatin, who became Secretary of the Treasury under Thomas Jefferson, states:

> The framers of the Constitution of the United States were deeply impressed with the still fresh recollection of the baneful effects of a paper money currency on the property and on the moral feeling of the community. It was accordingly provided by our National Charter that no State should coin money, emit bills of credit, make anything but gold and silver coin a tender in payment of debts, or pass any law impairing the obligation of contracts; and the power to coin money and to regulate the value thereof, and of foreign coin, was, by the same instrument, vested exclusively in Congress. As this body has no authority to make anything whatever a tender in payment of private debts, it necessarily follows

---

47. *The Madison Papers*, III (Washington, D.C., 1840), record of August 16, 1787, pp. 1343-46.

48. Ibid., p. 1346.

> that nothing but gold and silver coin can be made a legal tender for that purpose, and that Congress cannot authorize the payment in any specie of paper currency . . . debts . . . due the United States, or such debts of the United States as may, by special contract, be made payable in such paper. . . .
>
> The provisions of the Constitution were universally considered as affording a complete security against the danger of paper money. The introduction of the banking system met with a strenuous opposition on various grounds; but it was not apprehended that banknotes, convertible at will into specie, and which no person could be compelled to take in payment, would degenerate into pure paper money, no longer paid at sight in specie.[49]

Decades later, Daniel Webster commented similarly in favor of a pure specie standard of monetary policy, at least at the federal and state level:

> Most unquestionably there is no legal tender and there can be no legal tender in this country, under the authority of this government or any other, but gold and silver, either the coinage of our mints or foreign coin at rates regulated by Congress. This is a constitutional principle perfectly plain and of the very highest importance. The states are prohibited from making anything but gold and silver a tender in payment of debts, and although no such express prohibition is applied to Congress, yet as Congress has no power granted to it in this respect but to coin money and regulate the value of foreign coin, it clearly has no power to substitute paper or anything else for coin as a tender in payment of debts and in discharge of contracts.[50]

Thus, in short, the majority views at the Constitutional Convention were distinctly a hard money approach, supporting the concept of a 100 percent specie standard, at least as far as the government was concerned. Although the sentiment was clearly anti-

---

49. Albert Gallatin, *Writings*, edited by Henry Adams (New York, 1960), Vol. III, pp. 235-36. Gallatin's remarks were made in 1831, after serving office.

50. Daniel Webster, as quoted by Chief Justice Salmon P. Chase, "Supreme Court Reports," *Legal Tender Cases*, 12 Wall 586, Opinion of the Minority.

paper money, no effort was made at this time to prohibit paper issued by private banks. This was not a serious omission at the time, however, since banking in America was at its infancy in 1790. Only three banks had been established in the U.S. in the previous decade, the Bank of Pennsylvania, the Bank of New York, and the Massachusetts Bank, and these were "founded on specie."

Anti-Bank Sentiments in Early 19th Century

State-chartered banks proliferated in the 1790-1820 period of American history. By 1800 there were 28 commercial banks, and by 1811, there were 88. Early charters contained few provisions restricting a bank's activities, and by 1816, the number of state banks increased to nearly 250. Bank promoters expected high earnings and promoted speculative real estate and business ventures. The banks usually expanded their liabilities through the issuing of banknotes, which sharply increased following the War of 1812. Concerning this era, Rothbard writes, "These banks were primarily note-issuing institutions, generally run on loose principles. Little specie was paid in as capital, and it was quite common for the stockholders to pay for their bank stock with their own promissory notes, using the stock itself as the only collateral."[51]

Rapidly rising prices inevitably resulted, followed by a specie drain to the New England area to pay for importing supplies and textile manufactuing. Banks continued to expand banknotes, and it culminated in a suspension of specie payments outside the New England area in August 1814. Rapid note expansion renewed in 1815, while "suspension was considered a blessing by most bankers, for there was then no need to worry about the ratio of gold and silver reserves to liabilities."[52] Depression in later years, and the Panic of 1819, led to massive failures of banks in the West and South. In spite of this setback, banking remained popular

51. Murray N. Rothbard, *The Panic of 1819* (New York: Columbia University Press, 1962), p. 3.

52. Ross M. Robertson, *History of the American Economy* (New York: Harcourt, Brace & World, 1964), p. 161.

among businessmen and speculators. By 1834, there were more than 500 commercial banks in the United States.

It was during this early period of American history that the economic and banking views of the Jeffersonians and Jacksonians were formulated. These political leaders of the day, including many of the founding fathers, "wrote in full and sophisticated knowledge of classical economics and were fully devoted to capitalism and the free market, which they believed were hampered and not aided by the institution of fractional reserve banking."[53] Rothbard notes that during this period "America had quite a few exponents of the 'Currency Principle'—100 percent reserve banking and the idea that fiduciary bank credit causes a business cycle—several years before Thomas Joplin first gave it prominence in England. Perhaps one reason for this precedence was that Americans, while benefiting from the famous English bullionist discussions on problems of an inconvertible currency, were forced to grapple with inflation under a mostly convertible currency several years before the English—who did not complete their return to specie payments until 1821."[54]

Among the founding fathers who expressed a strong dislike for fractional reserve banking and favored a pure specie standard were Thomas Jefferson and John Adams. James Madison, who was sympathetic with hard money advocates, regarded paper money as theoretically superior to specie, but favored rigid limitations to its issue for fear of depreciation.

Jefferson was particularly adverse to *any* issue of paper currency. The Panic of 1819 confirmed Jefferson's suspicions of banking. He devised a plan, bluntly aimed at "the eternal suppression of bank paper," which he introduced in the Virginia legislature through his friend William C. Rives. It called for the complete withdrawal of banknotes in five years.[55] Jefferson concluded that

---

53. Murray N. Rothbard, *The Case for a 100 Percent Gold Dollar*, p. 35.

54. Rothbard, *The Panic of 1819*, p. 183.

55. Jefferson to William C. Rives, November 28, 1819, in his *Writings*, T. E. Bergh, ed., (Washington, D.C.: Jefferson Memorial Association of the United States, 1904), XV, pp. 229-32.

no government, state or federal, should be given the power to establish a bank or issue paper money. He supported a money currency consisting solely of specie.[56]

John Adams heartily agreed with his old opponent on this issue. Adams, in a letter to John Taylor of Caroline, strongly denounced banks and blamed them for the 1819-20 depression. He regarded the issue of paper beyond specie as "theft," and laden with economic disaster. He cited the example of Massachusetts in 1775, when paper money failed miserably and was quickly replaced by silver.[57] In a letter to Benjamin Rush in 1811, Adams called the banking system "downright corruption."[58] Also, he stated, "Every dollar of a bank bill that is issued beyond the quantity of gold and silver in the vaults represents nothing, and is therefore a cheat upon somebody."[59]

Adams' favorite book on economics, which was translated under the supervision of Thomas Jefferson, was by the French ideologue and economist Count Antoine Destutt de Tracy. De Tracy condemned paper money as theft and referred to banks as "radically vicious" organizations.[60]

John Adams' son, John Quincy Adams, had similar views on paper money during this period. While Secretary of State, he wrote a letter replying to a Frenchman, Peter Paul de Grand, and spoke highly of the old Amsterdam banking system, where paper was "always a representative and nothing more," equal to the amount of specie in the bank's vaults.[61]

---

56. Jefferson to Charles C. Pinckney, September 23, 1820, in ibid., XV, p. 279. Also, see Jefferson to Hugh Nelson, March 12, 1820, ibid., p. 258; and Jefferson to A. Gallatin, ibid., November 24, 1818; December 26, 1820.

57. John Adams to John Taylor, March 12, 1819, in Adams, *Works* (Boston: Little, Brown & Co., 1856), X, p. 375.

58. John Adams to Benjamin Rush, August 28, 1811, ibid., IX, p. 638.

59. Adams to F. A. Vanderkemp, February 16, 1809, ibid., IX, p. 610.

60. Michael J. L. O'Connor, *Origins of Academic Economics in the United States* (New York: Columbia University Press, 1944), p. 28. See also de Tracy, *Treatise on Political Economy* (Georgetown, Washington, D.C., 1817).

61. John Quincy Adams to Peter Paul Francis de Grand, November 16, 1818, *Writings*, Worthington C. Ford, ed., (New York: Macmillan, 1916), VI, pp. 472-73.

Virginia was a leading bastion of hard money views. Besides Thomas Jefferson, there was Governor Thomas Randolph, son-in-law and close friend of Jefferson, who strongly favored the use of gold as the nation's unit of account. According to Randolph, specie had relatively stable value, while bank credit created widespread fluctuations and eventual panic. He was not opposed to paper money per se, however, but only as long as it was absolutely convertible in specie and guaranteed to be equivalent to specie—in short, a 100 percent reserve system.[62]

Another notable Virginian favoring a pure specie program was Thomas Ritchie, editor of the Richmond *Enquirer*, who criticized inconvertible paper money and editorialized in favor of strict regulations over banking practices. Another Virginian, Spencer Roane, Chief Justice of the Virginia Court of Appeals, asserted that "banking is an evil of the first magnitude" and should be required to redeem in specie under all circumstances.[63]

One of the leading hard money economists of the time was Daniel Raymond, a Baltimore lawyer, who wrote the first systematic treatise on economics in the United States. Drawing on the specie-flow mechanism by David Hume, Raymond argued that bank credit raised domestic prices, promoted excessive speculation, and caused an unfavorable balance of trade. Ideally, he supported replacing banknotes with a national paper currency fully (100 percent) backed by specie. According to Raymond, issuing notes beyond specie was a "stupendous fraud."[64]

In Pennsylvania, one of the most prominent leaders of the pro-specie movement was Condy Raguet, an influential state senator. Raguet laid blame of the boom-bust cycle squarely on bank credit expansion. He also pioneered the view in the United States that deposits as well as notes constitute part of the money

62. Virginia General Assembly, *Journal of the House of Delegates, 1820-21* (December 4, 1820), pp. 11-12.

63. Murray N. Rothbard, *Panic of 1819*, pp. 137-40.

64. Daniel Raymond, *Elements of Political Economy* (Baltimore, Maryland: F. Luckas, Jr. and E. J. Coale, 1823), II, 132ff. Also, see ibid., I, pp. 248-53. His first edition (1820) was entitled *Thoughts on Political Economy.*

supply, a view the British Currency School failed to recognize, and a fact which eventually discredited the Peel Act of 1844. Raguet also viewed with strong suspicion all banks except those with 100 percent reserves for their demand liabilities.[65]

Other contemporary leaders who supported the anti-banking movement and a return to "sound" banking were Tennessee Representative Davy Crockett (who considered the whole banking system a "species of swindling on a large scale"), as well as Andrew Jackson, Martin Van Buren, Henry Harrison and James K. Polk, all of whom were later Presidents of the United States.

Many of the anti-bank, ultra-hard money advocates of the Jackson-Van Buren period were first converted to this view during the stormy banking era of the early 19th century. "Andrew Jackson himself foreshadowed his later opposition to banking by making himself the fervent leader of the opposition to inconvertible paper in Tennessee. Thomas Hart ("Old Bullion") Benton, later Jackson's hard money arm in the Senate, was converted to hard money by his experience with banking in Missouri during the panic. Future President James K. Polk of Tennessee, who was to be Jackson's leader in the House and later to establish the ultra hard money independent treasury system, began his political career in Tennessee in this period by urging return to specie payment. Amos Kendall, later Jackson's top adviser and confidant in the bank war, became an implacable enemy of banks during this period."[66]

Arguments against the overissue of notes and elasticity were generally related to specie outflow. "They (hard money advocates) declared that the banks first expanded the currency, thus causing rising prices and speculation, and that this fact caused an outflow of specie in the wake of which came contraction, business losses, and failures."[67] Thomas Law contended that "inasmuch as the

---

65. Pennsylvania Legislature, *Journal of the House*, 1820-21 (January 15, 1821), pp. 252-68. See also Condy Raguet, *A Treatise on Currency and Banking* (2nd ed., 1840), pp. 68-69, where he cites 100 percent reserve banks of Amsterdam and Hamburg.

66. Murray N. Rothbard, *Panic of 1819*, p. 188.

67. Lloyd W. Mints, *A History of Banking Theory* (Chicago, Illinois: University of Chicago Press, 1945), p. 157.

banks in some instances issued notes to the extent of five times the amount of specie held, notes would have to be contracted in the ratio of five to one for specie withdrawn."[68] Henry Vethake pointed out that a purely metallic standard would result only in a "one-to-one contraction" of the money supply.[69]

In the early 1830s, William M. Gouge wrote favorably on the "hard-money banks," using the Bank of Hamburg as a model. Convertibility was not sufficient to avoid perverse fluctuations in credit. He believed in a return to the hard money banks. These banks would be required to carry 100 percent reserves behind demand deposits and could lend no more than the amount of their capital.[70]

The Anti-Banking Movement During the 1830s

The debate over the rechartering of the U.S. National Bank raised a number of key issues regarding monetary policy and hard currency. Philosophically, Jackson held to the view that the "constitutional money" of specie, not paper, should be restored. He vetoed the recharter bill in 1832 and removed the national bank's deposits to selected state banks in 1833.

Many of Jackson's supporters pushed for the elimination of small banknotes, arguing that banknotes drive out specie. William Gouge, originator of the idea, wanted notes up to $100 to be eliminated gradually over a 10-year period. Gallatin and other monetary experts supported this measure, but it met with little success. Most, however, did *not* favor elimination of all notes, but only small ones. "The ardent exponents never thought of an exclusively specie currency," notes Dorfman.[71] But eliminating small notes would supposedly go far in preventing panic and cyclical fluctuations.

---

68. Thomas Law, *Address before the Columbian Institute in 1825* (published in 1828), p. 67.

69. Henry Vethake, *The Principles of Political Economy* (1838), p. 181.

70. William M. Gouge, *A Short History of Paper Money and Banking in the United States* (New York: B. & S. Collins, 1835), pp. 21-22, 172.

71. Joseph Dorfman, *The Economic Mind in American Civilization* (New York: The Viking Press, 1949), Vol. II, p. 609.

In July, 1836, Jackson issued his famous specie circular barring banknotes from use in buying public lands in the West in an effort to reduce speculative fever and restore the "constitutional currency." Instead, it precipitated the Panic of 1837. President Martin Van Buren blamed the crisis on "excessive issues of paper and by other facilities for the acquisition and enlargement of credit."[72]

Others viewed the depression differently. There was strong congressional opposition to the "hard money" line, which was regarded by many as pro-rich, anti-labor, and far too restrictive. They felt that a return to specie had extremely harmful deflationary effects. The judicious use of inconvertible currency and credit is "necessary" during wartime in order to ease the financial burdens over a long period of time.[73]

Following the Panic of 1837, the opposition to banking became so strong in some areas that several states absolutely outlawed banks for a period.[74] The Loco-Focos were members of the Equal Rights Party, the most prominent of labor parties in New York during the 1830-40 period. As supporters of Jackson, they favored the abolition of small bank notes and of usury laws, and supported the New York Restraining Act, which forbade deposit and discounting functions of banks.

John Vethake, M.D., was the most flamboyant leader of the Loco-Focos and a member of the "Anti-Monopoly Democrats." He strongly denounced chartered corporations and monopolies of the state. The Loco-Focos were a minority and formed their own state party in 1836. For governor, they nominated the Buffalo merchant Isaac S. Smith, who regarded the term "paper money" an absurdity, and favored specie as the only proper circulating medium.

William Leggett, journalist of the *New York Evening Post*, was their most influential leader during the Panic of 1837. Under his leadership, the Loco-Focos sought to eliminate the banknotes of

72. Quoted in Dorfman, *The Economic Mind*, II, p. 613.

73. Ibid., II, p. 614.

74. Harry E. Miller, *Banking Theories in the United States Before 1860* (Cambridge, Massachusetts: Harvard University Press, 1927), p. 21.

distant banks. They issued a manifesto against high food prices and recommended that "workingmen" refuse paper money or demand immediate redemption of all notes, which they thought would reduce prices. The "Loco-Foco Resolution" of the Equal Rights Party read: "Resolved—That the true remedy for the people, which will reduce the price of all the necessaries of life, is that every workingman refuse paper money in payment for his services, or demand specie of the banks for all notes paid to him." Speaking of the breadth of this movement, William Trimble writes, "The national Locofocoism identified itself with its local prototype in New York, moreover, in regarding the banking interests as then constituted in this country as a bulwark of privilege similar to that of the feudal nobility in Europe. The pith of the progressive Democracy's opposition to the credit system was the issuance by the banks of a currency not strictly redeemable in specie."[75]

In the early 1840s, James Cox, who favored a purely metallic currency, concurred with Condy Raguet that deposits and notes served the same as currency. He noted the convenience of the paper notes over the "cumbersome" and "costly" nature of specie, but in spite of these inconveniences, he favored the return of metallic money.[76]

The British Currency School

The Currency School in England developed during the debates over convertibility, resumption of specie payments, and the role of the Bank of England during the 1820-1840 period. The "currency principle" was first pronounced by Thomas Joplin in 1826.[77] Other

---

75. William Trimble, "Diverging Tendencies in New York Democracy in the Period of the Locofocos," *American Historical Review*, #3, April 1919. See also Fitzwilliam Byrdsall, *History of the Loco-Foco or Equal Rights Party* (New York, 1842). On William Leggett, see *A Collection of the Political Writings of William Leggett*, edited by Theodore Sedgewick, Jr., (New York, 1840).

76. James Cox, *Metallic Money, Its Value and Its Function* (Philadelphia, Pennsylvania: Office of the Public Ledger, 1841), pp. 8-14. A. A. A. Gallatin also favored the 100 percent standard: See *Considerations, Etc.* (1831), p. 38.

77. Thomas Joplin, *An Essay on the General Principles and Present Practice of Banking in England and Scotland* (London: Baldwin, 1826).

members of the school of thought who elaborated on Joplin's views were Samuel Jones Loyd, George Ward Norman, and Robert Torrens. Loyd was a banker and member of Parliament (1819-1826); Norman was also a banker, who popularized the terms "currency" and "banking" principles; and Torrens was a retired colonel and member of Parliament (1831-1835). "Their cardinal tenet was that, to safeguard the value of the standard, the quantity of paper money and coin in circulation should never be allowed to differ from the amount of money which would circulate if the currency were entirely metallic."[78] The Currency School, though recognizing certain defects in the use of specie as money, held up gold and silver as ideal. To quote Norman: "I consider a metallic currency to be the most perfect currency, except so far as respects inconvenience, in some respects, and cost. In everything else a metallic currency is the most perfect, and should be looked upon as the type of all other currencies."[79]

The school was heavily influenced by the early writings of David Ricardo, who argued in 1810 for the resumption of specie payments by the Bank of England. Ricardo's solution was stated as follows: "The remedy which I propose for all the evils in our currency, is that the Bank should gradually decrease the amount of their notes in circulation until they shall have rendered the remainder of equal value with the coins which they represent, or, in other words, till the prices of gold and silver bullion should be brought down to their Mint price."[80] Ricardo recognized the "most disastrous consequences to the trade and commerce of the country" as a result of this deflationary measure, but argued that this was the "only means of restoring our currency to its just and equitable value." If this policy were enforced gradually, there would be "little inconvenience," contended Ricardo. He never explicitly proposed a 100 percent specie standard for England, but

78. A. E. Feaveryear, *The Pound Sterling*, p. 244. See also Lloyd W. Mints, *A History of Banking Theory*, p. 75.

79. Quoted in F. A. Walker, *Money* (New York: H. Holt, 1891), p. 420.

80. David Ricardo, *The Works of David Ricardo* (London: John Murray, 1876), p. 287.

rather favored simple convertibility. As long as the price of bullion remained the same value as the banknotes they represent, he appeared to have no objection to their expansion beyond specie. But the Bank should have no discretionary power: "The issuers of paper money should regulate their issues solely by the price of bullion, and never by the quantity of their paper in circulation."[81]

The founders of the Currency School adopted this view of Ricardo: "The writers of the currency school explicitly and strongly opposed any discretionary management of the currency."[82] A severe deflationary measure to reduce the bank's notes and coin equal to a 100 percent standard was rejected, however, on the basis of political infeasibility. The Peel Act of 1844, strongly endorsed by the school, called for all *future* issues of money and currency (coins and notes) to increase or decrease equal to increases or decreases in the country's bullion, without deviation. The chief aim or direction of the Peel Act was to achieve a pure gold standard, but only over a lengthy period of time. It did not establish a pure standard in one sweeping decree. Thus, noting that the currency principle required the full backing of notes by bullion (i.e., bullion certificates), Peel's Bank Charter Act of 1844 "did not follow strictly the currency principle."[83]

The failure of the Peel Act did not lie in some kind of fatal weakness in a pure 100 percent specie standard, but inevitably in the failure of its supporters to comprehend the nature of bank deposits and the creation of a fractional reserve system. While easily accepting notes and coin with the attributes of money, they regarded other money substitutes, such as circulating bills of exchange, deposits and checks as merely "auxiliary currency," not real money, and therefore, not subject to the same restrictions.

The "currency" advocates were well aware of the existence of checking accounts, noting that many banks no longer even issue notes, but unfortunately they did not regard them as money per se.[84]

---

81. Ibid., p. 403.
82. Lloyd W. Mints, *A History of Banking Theory*, p. 77.
83. A. E. Feaveryear, *The Pound Sterling*, p. 253.
84. Ibid., p. 249-50.

Norman, for example, "greatly underestimated the importance of deposits."[85] Loyd denied that they were money: "A Bank of Issue is entrusted with the *creation* of the circulating medium. A Bank of Deposit and Discount is concerned only with the *use, distribution, or application* of that circulating medium."[86] Apparently, these men failed to see the mechanism by which fractional reserve banking can create fiduciary money through the loan or discount system. Thus, the "failure to recognize the essential similarity of banknotes and bank deposits" doomed the efforts of the Currency School to establish a pure gold standard in England.[87]

The Banking School, led by Thomas Tooke, John Fullerton, and James Wilson, in opposition to the Peel Act and the Currency School, fully recognized the economic power of the banks' deposits and their ability to create money. They considered the currency principle as unnecessary government interference in the banking system. Instead, the Banking School favored "free banking" as long as convertibility was maintained. In the words of Sir Henry Parnell, a defender of free banking, "It is this continual demand for coin, by the banks on one another, that gives the principle of convertibility full effect, and no such thing as an excess of paper or as a depreciation of its value can take place for want of a sufficiently early and active demand for gold."[88]

Parnell and other members of the Banking School pointed to the sound structure of the Scottish banks, which were highly competitive and were accustomed to frequent redemption of country banknotes into specie.[89] In summary, banking should be "wholly free from all legislative interference," including reserve requirements. Under the circumstances, while maintaining convertibility,

---

85. Lloyd W. Mints, *A History of Banking Theory*, p. 79.

86. S. J. Loyd, *Reflections Suggested by a Perusal of Mr. J. Horsley Palmer's Pamphlet on the Causes and Consequences of the Pressure on the Money Market* (1837), p. 43.

87. Ludwig von Mises, *The Theory of Money and Credit*, p. 369.

88. Sir Henry Parnell, "Observations on Paper Money, Banking and Overtrading, including those parts of the evidence taken before the Committee of the House of Commons which explained the Scotch System of Banking," Pamphlet (1827), p. 88.

89. Adam Smith, who favored "free banking," wrote favorably on the Scottish system. See *The Wealth of Nations*, pp. 281-82.

the overissue of notes was impossible. This view did not suggest a 100 percent reserve system, however. On the contrary, the Banking School argued that a partial reserve system, tempered by a high degree of competition, provided the necessary "elasticity" to adjust favorably to the needs of business and trade.

Economic Thought During the Civil War Period

From the late 1850s to the 1880s, hard money economists in the U.S. were primarily preoccupied with domestic monetary problems surrounding the Civil War period. The problems of an "ideal" monetary standard were laid aside by the realities of the new greenbacks and the free silver movement. Though they commented from time to time on the currency reform movement in England, "the pre-Civil War demand for currency of 'hard money'. . . virtually disappeared."[90]

Nevertheless, a few economic observers continued to write about the problems of hard currency reform. Boston merchant Charles H. Carroll was the foremost hard money advocate to write in the late 1850s and 1860s. Writing frequently in *Hunt's Merchants' Magazine*, Carroll argued in favor of "bullion banking," requiring 100 percent backing of demand liabilities with specie or full-bodied coins. He advocated that the monetary unit of account be changed from the dollar, which was a source of "false monetary ideas," to a troy ounce of gold or silver. Only full-bodied coins, with a weight and fineness specified, and fully backed coin certificates should circulate as currency, according to Carroll. Carroll was sharply critical of fractional reserve paper money. Currency created out of "bank debt" was called a "fatal principle," causing high prices and high interest rates. He blamed the Bank of England for introducing fractional reserve banking, but lauded France for sticking to the use of gold coins.[91]

---

90. Lloyd W. Mints, *A History of Banking Theory*, pp. 212-13.

91. Charles Holt Carroll, *Organization of Debt Into Currency and Other Papers* (Princeton, New Jersey: D. Van Nostrand Co., 1964), Edward C. Simmons, ed., pp. xi-xiv. See also Carroll, "The Currency and the Tariff," *Hunt's Merchants' Magazine and Commercial Review*, XXXIII (August, 1855), pp. 1919-99; in ibid., p. 12.

During this period, Stephen A. Colwell criticized fractional reserves, noting that this was an unacceptable state of circumstances because banks' assets could not be sufficiently liquid to cover large redemptions of notes and deposits. Consequently, he proposed two separate accounts—"one for money, and one for credit."[92] Money would be redeemable on demand. "Banknotes payable on demand should never be issued beyond the amount of specie actually in the bank," Colwell emphasized.[93] Credit, on the other hand, would be redeemable only at the time the loan became due.

General Amasa Walker, "an outstanding figure in the financial, political, and academic worlds," during the Civil War period, was one of the most thoroughgoing critics of fractional reserve banking, which he called the "mixed currency" system. His popular book, *The Science of Wealth*, contains lengthy arguments against fractional reserve banking. As an alternative, he wrote favorably of the ancient "banks of deposit" in Italy, Amsterdam and Hamburg, which dealt in "mercantile currency."[94]

Walker was unalterably opposed to inconvertible paper money. Free banking should be permitted, Walker reasoned, as long as "only notes equivalent to so much coin are issued" and that "no issues should be made except upon specie in hand."[95] Banks would be allowed to "discount" funds of people who wished to lend money, but this function would be separate from that of deposits. They could also "issue notes for circulation" at 100 percent reserves. Thus, Walker spoke properly of a "bank of deposit, discount, and circulation," but not of a "mixed currency bank."[96] Regarded by Dorfman as his "most significant contribution on monetary matters," Walker felt that *deposits* were far more impor-

---

92. Stephen A. Colwell, *The Ways and Means of Payment* (2nd ed., 1860), p. 493. Cf. pp. 482-83, 488, 632.

93. Ibid., p. 495; 11-12, 368.

94. Amasa Walker, *The Science of Wealth*, pp. 184-223. See also Dorfman, *The Economic Mind*, Vol. III, pp. 50-54.

95. Ibid., p. 231.

96. Amasa Walker, *Nature and Uses of Money and Mixed Currency* (Boston: Crosly, Nichols & Co., 1857), pp. 20-21, 52.

tant than banknotes in causing suspicion of specie and a collapse of credit and loan demand.[97]

General Walker, along with Charles H. Carroll, Gamaliel Bradford, Henry Bronson, and F. A. Walker (first president of the American Economic Association and Amasa Walker's son) all approved of the Peel Act of 1844 in England, but criticized it for not going far enough to include deposits as well as notes.[98]

During this period, on the Continent, two German economists, Philip Joseph Geyer and J. L. Tellkampf, adhered to the "very strictest currency doctrine," looking upon banknotes "only as a more convenient form in which money can be carried about or transported."[99] Geyer, in particular, distinguished between fully covered and uncovered banknotes. Only fully covered note issues are a "real" economic factor of production, according to Geyer, while uncovered notes are "artificial" capital and subject the economy to a cyclical behavior. He opposed granting banks the freedom of note issue, but was in favor of deposit banking. Geyer was critical of the Peel Act "because it did not carry the currency principle to its logical conclusion. It should either forbid uncovered notes altogether or else arrange that they should be equal to the idea of money capital. Since it did neither of these things it could not prevent crises. . . ."[100]

One of the few U.S. government officials to favor a pure specie standard following the Civil War was Isaiah W. Sylvester, an officer in the U.S. Assay Office in New York. In a pamphlet, *Bullion Certificates as Currency*, Sylvester proposed that gold bars be made legal tender. Paper certificates of the bullion would be issued from a value of $1 to $1,000. These certificates would be

---

97. Dorfman, *The Economic Mind*, Vol. III, p. 54.

98. See Gamaliel Bradford, "Lombard and Wall Streets," *North American Review* XIX (1874), pp. 333, 342, 355; and "Three Systems of Currency," *Transactions of the National Association for the Promotion of Social Science* (1875), pp. 677-79. Henry Bronson, *The Money Problem* (1877), p. 15. F. A. Walker, *Money* (New York: H. Holt, 1891), pp. 470-71.

99. Vera Smith, *The Rationale of Central Banking* (London: King, 1936), p. 112.

100. Ibid., p. 111. See also Philip Joseph Geyer, *Banken und Krisen* (1865), pp. 33ff.

backed 100 percent by the bullion bars, which would be certified by weight and fineness. Sylvester also favored using silver bars as legal tender, but they would be priced in terms of gold bars, fluctuating according to supply and demand. In essence, a parallel standard, as opposed to the more common bimetallic standard, would be established.[101] However, Sylvester's proposal apparently received little attention in Washington.

Pure Specie Standard During the 20th Century

During the 20th century, monetary policy has been chiefly oriented toward the mechanics of a fractional reserve paper money system, with gold given prominence in international affairs. The gold exchange standard, where central banks exchange gold bullion at fixed rates, collapsed in 1933 due to strong deflationary forces in the Western world.

During these times of monetary and social upheaval, "ideal" economic programs are often envisioned and proposed. It was during the Great Depression of the 1930s, for example, that Irving Fisher (and later the Chicago School) advanced the concept of rules versus authority and its ideal monetary system of a 100 percent fiat paper standard.

Fisher's 100 percent plan was by no means a pure commodity standard, however. In fact, he regarded gold as "unstable." Nevertheless, his 100 percent rule incorporated many of the criticisms of the modern banking system that were propagated by the gold standard school of thought. Fisher, in defending his program, wrote that the 100 percent program was "a return from the present extraordinary and ruinous system of lending the same money 8 or 10 times over, to the conservative safety deposit system of the old goldsmiths, before they began lending out improperly what was entrusted to them for safekeeping. It was this abuse of trust which, after being accepted as standard practice, evolved into modern deposit banking. From the standpoint of public policy it

---

101. Isaiah W. Sylvester, *Bullion Certificates as Currency* (New York: U.S. Assay Office, 1882).

is still an abuse, no longer an abuse of trust but an abuse of the loan and deposit functions."[102] Fisher also compared the fall of the Bank of Amsterdam to present banking: ". . . the only important difference between the abuse which ultimately wrecked the Bank of Amsterdam and the modern way of lending depositors' money (which has nearly wrecked capitalistic civilization) is that the modern system is not secret but is practiced openly, with the consent of all concerned, and is supposedly safeguarded by legal or other restrictions, especially as to reserves."[103]

Henry C. Simons of Chicago, highly sympathetic to Fisher's plan, offered a strong critique of modern banking practices and fractional reserves. According to Simons, fractional reserve banking is highly unstable: "We have reached a situation where private bank credit represents all but a small fraction of our total effective circulating medium. This gives us an economy in which significant disturbances of equilibrium set in motion forces which operate grossly to aggravate, rather than to correct, the initial maladjustments." Again, in a footnote, Simons elaborated: "There is likely to be extreme economic instability under any financial system where *the same funds* are made to serve as *investment funds for industry and trade* and as *the liquid cash reserves of individuals*. Our financial structure has been built largely on the illusion that funds can at the same time be both available and invested—and this observation applies to our savings banks (and in lesser degree to many other financial institutions) as well as commercial, demand deposit banking."[104]

Fisher and Simons both regarded the gold standard as unstable under a fractional reserve system. Fisher noted: "A gold standard, in the sense of an unlimited liability to redeem paper money

---

102. Irving Fisher, *100% Money* (New Haven, Connecticut: The City Printing Co., 1945), pp. 18-19.

103. Ibid., pp. 35-36. As a matter of comparison, Knut Wicksell proposed earlier a similiar monetary system, based entirely on credit, which he called a "pure credit system." See Wicksell, *Lectures on Political Economy* (New York: Macmillan, 1935), pp. 87-122.

104. Henry C. Simons, *Economic Policy for a Free Society*, pp. 55, 320n.

in gold, is analogous, in its destabilizing influence, to the 10% system [fractional reserve banking], with its unlimited liability to redeem check book money in pocketbook money. We have one inverted pyramid under another with a tiny apex of gold at the bottom."[105] Simons corroborated this view:

> The penultimate step away from the ideal financial system carries us to one under which all matured (demand) and maturing obligations are legally convertible into some particular commodity like gold, whose total available supply is only a trivial fraction of the amounts which creditors are in a position to demand. And, finally, the worst financial structure is realized when many nations, with similar financial practices and institutions and similar credit pyramids (and narrowly nationalist commercial policies), adopt the same commodity as the monetary standard. When one thinks of the total potential creditor demands for gold for hoarding, in and after 1929, it seems almost beyond diabolical ingenuity to conceive a financial system better designed for our economic destruction.[106]

The Fisher idea consisted of 100 percent reserve banking of a fiduciary medium tied to a commodity index. It was fairly popular during the 1930s and early 1940s, and was commented on by economists and political observers, but gradually faded in popularity as relative stability returned to the banking system and federal deposit insurance took root.[107]

Though the Western monetary system was moving further and further from gold as a central monetary standard, there were numerous voices who continued the hard money tradition. Most wanted a return to the pre-1933 gold exchange standard and the reinstatement of convertibility as a sufficient condition and deter-

---

105. Irving Fisher, *100% Money*, p. 188.

106. Henry C. Simons, *Economic Policy*, p. 168.

107. See A. G. Hart, "The 'Chicago Plan' of Banking Reform," *Review of Economic Studies*, II (1934-35), pp. 104-16. James W. Angell, "The 100 Per Cent Reserve Plan," *Quarterly Journal of Economics*, L (1935-36), I-35. Frank D. Graham, "Partial Reserve Money and the 100 Per Cent Proposal," *American Economic Review*, XXVI (1936), pp. 428-40. Henry C. Simons, *A Positive Program for Laissez Faire* (Chicago: University of Chicago, 1934), pp. 18, 23-24.

rent to inflationary economic policies of Western governments. These advocates included Walter E. Spahr and the Economists' National Committee on Monetary Policy, Ludwig von Mises, Henry Hazlitt, Lionel Robbins, Jacques Rueff, Melchior Palyi, and Hans Sennholz, among many others.[108] Contrasting their views with the pure 100 percent gold standard, Friedman notes that the 100 percent system

> . . . is not the system supported by most current proponents of the gold standard nor is it the system that prevailed even during the halcyon days of the gold standard in the nineteenth century, when there were large admixtures of fiduciary elements and much conscious management. It is even farther from the nominal gold standard that prevailed in the United States from World War I to 1933, let alone since 1934. During that period we have had none of the advantages of a full-fledged gold standard, and many of its disadvantages greatly exaggerated.[109]

One of the few advocates of a full-fledged gold standard was economist Elgin Groseclose, who wrote in the 1930s and 1940s, and favored a 100 percent gold standard chiefly from a moral point of view. He regarded the practice of the goldsmiths of "using deposited funds to their own interest and profit" as "essentially unsound, if not actually dishonest and fraudulent."[110] Mixing the deposit and money creation functions was, according to Groseclose, perpetuating the falsehood that "we can eat our cake and have it." He advocated abandoning the present banking structure of fractional reserves and replacing it with 100 percent deposit and investment banking.

---

108. See Walter E. Spahr and James Washington Bell, eds., *A Proper Monetary and Banking System for the United States* (New York: Ronald Press, 1960). Henry Hazlitt, *What You Should Know About Inflation* (New York: Funk & Wagnalls, 1965), pp. 58-61. Jacques Rueff, *The Monetary Sin of the West* (New York: Macmillan, 1972). Hans Sennholz, *Inflation or Gold Standard?* (Lansing, Mich.: Constitutional Alliance, 1975).

109. Milton Friedman, *Monetary Stability*, p. 81.

110. Elgin Groseclose, *Money and Man* (New York: Frederick Ungar, 1961), p. 178. Originally published under the title, *Money: The Human Conflict* (1934).

Professor F. A. Hayek, writing in the 1930s, was also highly sympathetic with a pure 100 percent gold standard, and tried to demonstrate the superiority of such a monetary system over the mixed, fractional reserve gold standard of the time. Hayek stated, in close proximity to the currency principle, "A possible, although perhaps somewhat fantastic, solution would seem to be to reduce proportionately the gold equivalents of all the different national monetary units to such an extent that all the money in all countries could be covered 100 percent by gold, and from that point onwards to allow variations in the national circulation only in proportion to changes in the quantity of gold in the country."[111] In this context, Hayek considers the economics of a "purely metallic currency," where there are two countries, both using metallic coins which "are freely and without cost interchangeable at the mints." Under this model, Hayek develops the international economics of such a system and shows how it would be a stable system. When changes in demand for trade take place, "It will be prices and incomes of particular individuals and particular industries which will be affected and the effects will not be essentially different from those which will follow any shifts of demand between different industries or localities."[112] Regarding the real world problem of specie outflows, Hayek's cure appears to be 100 percent reserves: "The only real cure would be if the reserves kept were large enough to allow them to vary by the full amount by which the total circulation of the country might possibly change, that is, if the principle of Peel's Act of 1844 could be applied to all forms of money, including in particular bank deposits."[113]

In the end, however, Hayek concluded that such a plan would be "somewhat impractical," adding though that it would be a move "in the right direction."[114] Major defects of the gold standard, even in its pure form, would be sudden changes in produc-

111. F. A. Hayek, *Monetary Nationalism and International Stability* (New York: Longmans, Green, 1937), pp. 81-82.

112. Ibid., pp. 4-9, 20-34.

113. Ibid., p. 33.

114. Ibid., p. 83.

tion or the demand for gold, and the problem of bank evasion and the uncanny ability of banks to escape the 100 percent rule imposed on them.

In more recent times, Hayek abandoned the pure gold standard entirely on behalf of a composite commodity standard, where the stock of money would expand or contract according to a raw commodity index.[115] Later, in the 1970s he advocated the "denationalization" of government monopoly of money and the competitive circulation of privately issued currency.[116]

Another well-known economist to offer a sympathetic ear to a pure commodity standard is Professor Milton Friedman. In his chapter, "Why Should Government Intervene in Monetary and Banking Questions?" in *A Program for Monetary Stability*, Friedman asked basic questions about money created through the market versus government decree. As in most economic matters, Friedman is sceptical of government interference: "Control over monetary and banking arrangements is a particularly dangerous power to entrust to government because of its far reaching effects on economic activity at large—as numerous episodes from ancient times to the present and over the whole globe tragically demonstrate. And Friedman is therefore "by no means certain that the government should control money."[117]

Friedman, in philosophical agreement with Fisher and Simons, charges that the present banking system is "inherently unstable." He states: "For a given total of high-powered money in existence, a decision by a holder of money to convert deposits into currency tends to produce a decline in the total stock of money; a decision to convert currency into deposits, a rise." The same problem exists with shifts among different types of deposits with differ-

---

115. F. A. Hayek, "A Commodity Reserve Currency," *Individualism and Economic Order* (Chicago: University of Chicago Press, 1948), pp. 209-19.

116. Hayek, *The Denationalization of Money* (London: The Institute of Economic Affairs, 1976). For a critique of Hayek's commodity index and denationalization proposals, see Rothbard, "The Case for a Genuine Gold Dollar," in *The Gold Standard*, edited by Llewellyn H. Rockwell, Jr. (Lexington, Mass: Lexington Books, 1985), pp. 2-7.

117. Milton Friedman, *Monetary Stability*, p. 4.

ent legal reserve requirements. The Federal Reserve has tried to implement "compensating changes," but without success, according to Friedman.[118]

As an alternative to this "unstable" system, Friedman seriously considers the market solution of a "pure commodity standard," where all monetary units consist of physical units of a commodity or literal warehouse receipts for the commodity. With respect to a "full-fledged gold standard," Friedman states: "A full-fledged gold standard in which all money consisted of gold or warehouse receipts for gold except perhaps for a fixed fiduciary issue would have the great merits of complete automaticity and freedom from governmental control." But, at the same time, Friedman points out that such a standard "would be costly in terms both of resources used to mine gold and of the price movements resulting from changes in the relative cost of producing gold and other commodities."[119] Due to these cost factors, as well as lack of widespread support in Western society for a pure standard, Friedman rejects a 100 percent gold standard.

Elsewhere, Friedman elaborates:

> If an automatic commodity standard were feasible, it would provide an excellent solution to the liberal dilemma of how to get a stable monetary framework without the danger of irresponsible exercise of monetary powers. A full commodity standard, for example, an honest-to-goodness gold standard in which 100 percent of the money consisted literally of gold, widely supported by a public imbued with the mythology of a gold standard and the belief that it is immoral and improper for government to interfere with its operation, would provide an effective control against governmental tinkering with the currency and against irresponsible monetary action. Under such a standard, any monetary powers of government would be very minor in scope.[120]

The high cost of gold production, however, provides a strong

---

118. Ibid., pp. 67-68.

119. Ibid., p. 81.

120. Milton Friedman, "Should There be an Independent Monetary Authority?" in Yeager, ed., *Monetary Constitution*, pp. 221-22.

incentive to introduce fiduciary elements, according to Friedman. Consequently, he states,

> My conclusion is that an automatic commodity standard is neither feasible nor a desirable solution to the problem of establishing monetary arrangements for a free society. It is not desirable because it would involve a large cost in the form of resources used to produce the monetary commodity. It is not feasible because the mythology and beliefs required to make it effective do not exist.[121]

Instead of a pure commodity standard, Friedman joins with Irving Fisher and others in advocating a 100 percent fiduciary standard under the Federal Reserve System.[122]

Renaissance of the 100 Percent Specie Standard?

Recent economic experience in the Western world has renewed interest in the 100 percent idea as a monetary tool and economic system. The inflationary recession of the 1970's and early 1980's, the worst declines in economic activity worldwide since the Great Depression in the 1930's, and the recent concurrence of high rates of price inflation and unemployment, coupled with the succession of monetary and foreign exchange crises, has led to a reexamination of fundamental neoclassical principles of monetary and fiscal economics.

The most prominent economist in recent years to proclaim a strict full-fledged specie standard is Professor Murray N. Rothbard, whose writings have become increasingly popular among hard money believers and investors. In his 1962 contribution to Leland B. Yeager's compilation of papers *In Search of a Monetary Constitution*, which included views of James M. Buchanan, Milton Friedman, and Arthur Kemp, Rothbard first wrote in support of "the complete, uninhibited gold standard," despite its lack of pop-

121. Ibid., pp. 223-24.

122. Milton Friedman, "How 100% Reserves Would Work," in Yeager, *Monetary Constitution*, pp. 69-70.

ularity among economists at the time.[123] He not only advocated the use of gold as a basis of international transactions, but also for a "genuine gold standard at home." He was highly critical of "the hardy band of current advocates of the gold standard, who called for a virtual restoration of the status quo *ante* 1933," which Rothbard viewed as having fatal flaws which "contributed signally to its final breakdown in 1933."[124]

In proposing the idea of 100 percent specie as a monetary standard of the world, Rothbard's aim is to frame "a monetary policy . . . truly compatible with the free market in its widest and fullest sense," and herein he argued that only a 100 percent, fully backed, specie-money could be compatible. Rothbard takes a purely laissez faire position in monetary affairs, maintaining that money can be totally free from government manipulation. This is to a large extent a break from tradition. Although traditional adherents to the pure gold standard have largely been in favor of a limited role by government in monetary affairs, most have supported various measures aimed at strengthening the market system of money. These roles include guarantees of fineness and weight, prohibiting and discouraging fraud, and so on. In addition, most have opposed private coinage.

Rothbard's thesis is particularly relevant to this period of monetary history because of his contention that the fractional reserve system is largely responsible for the inflationary recessions of the recent past, or at least creates the environment by which an "inflationary recession" can take place. Following up on the views of Simons and Friedman regarding the "unstable" nature of modern banking, Rothbard contends that fractional reserve banking, coupled with increases in fiduciary issues, creates a boom-bust cycle.

---

123. "The Case for the 100 Per Cent Gold Dollar," in Yeager, ed., *Monetary Constitution*. See also his article in *The Gold Standard, op. cit.* pp. 1-17. And Rothbard, *The Mystery of Banking* (New York: Richardson and Snyder, 1983), pp. 249-269.

124. "The Case for the 100 Per Cent Gold Dollar," p. 1.

Summary

The world's monetary system began with commodity-money, formulated over the centuries in the marketplace. Ultimately the precious metals of gold and silver, in the form of bullion or full-bodied coins, became the principal universal commodity-money.

Gradually, token coins, paper notes, and bank deposits were introduced into the monetary framework. Originally these new issues served as "representative money" or warehouse receipts for the actual bullion or coin on deposit, and did not exceed the quantity of metal they represented. It was not long, however, before these quasi-monies were issued far in excess of the metal they represented, thus introducing fiduciary elements into the monetary system for the first time.

In the case of bank deposits and the checking system, the fiduciary method was indirect and unrecognized at first. The goldsmiths, accustomed to lending funds, were the first bankers to mix the deposit and lending functions. Because of the fungible nature of money, the legal system was unable to recognize the unique nature of bank money and consequently gave tacit approval of fractional reserve banking.

The legal sanctioning of this fundamental banking practice did not, however, relieve the economic crises which beset the Western world, nor did it end the search for a stable monetary environment. It was during these critical economic disturbances that reform movements, such as the 100 percent specie proposal, captured the minds of many political and economic thinkers of the day. Hard money advocates blamed the banks for speculative booms and financial depressions, and called for a return to a "sound" bullion standard, where banknotes and deposits were backed by 100 percent specie.

Like other "ideal" monetary reforms, the 100 percent specie standard was most often espoused or revived during times of monetary upheaval—as, for example, during the European banking crises of the early 17th century, when the Continental "banks of deposit" were established; during the American economic panics of the early 19th century, when the Jacksonians and the Jeffersonians led the "anti-bank" movement; during the English debates over specie resumption and the role of the Bank of England, when the Currency School fought for the enactment of the Peel Act of 1844; during the Civil War-greenback period of American history, when hard money adherents wrote lengthy articles and books in favor of 100 percent banking; during the Great Depression of the 1930s, when Hayek, Fisher and Simons promoted the advantages of 100 percent reserve banking; and most recently, during the 1970s-1980s economic crises, when the hard-money camp led a revival of a pure gold dollar concept. In all these cases, historical events have led to a reform movement favoring some kind of ideal monetary standard. But equally important, these ideal standards always seemed to fade into obscurity as economic conditions improved.

3

Elements of a Pure Specie Standard

The operations of a 100 percent specie standard have evolved over the years and by no means appear monolithic as perceived by its advocates. Differences, however, seem to be over mechanics rather than the fundamental principles behind the 100 percent framework.

The Fundamental Principle

The underlying principle adopted by the Currency School and other hard money proponents throughout the gold standard tradition has been this: that money should consist wholly of a full-bodied commodity, and that all money substitutes are simply claims equivalent to an equal amount of money commodity. However, the choice of specie, or gold and silver bullion, as the basic money, is not an arbitrary one. Gold is adopted as the appropriate unit of account because of its natural emergence as the most efficient money in the competitive marketplace, displacing all other previously used commodities over the centuries. The 100 percent adherents regard their monetary standard as a consistent market approach to monetary matters.

Reflecting the views of the hard money school of thought, General Amasa Walker refers to gold and silver as stable in value, conveniently portable, malleable, of uniform quality, indestructible, universally appreciated, generally diffused, sufficiently plentiful, and inconsumable by use.[1] These characteristics of gold and

1. Amasa Walker, *Science of Wealth*, pp. 127-29.

and silver, according to Walker, prove to make them far superior as money over all the other metals or commodities.

Monetary Unit of Account

Gold has been the traditionally premier money, while other metals such as silver and copper have been useful for small transactions. Gold being the highest priced monetary unit per troy ounce since the beginning of a metallic standard, it was natural that eventually it became the monetary unit of account or *numeraire* among Western nations. In fact, most national currencies on the gold standard eventually defined their currency in specified weights of gold bullion.

Several hard money advocates, such as Charles H. Carroll, J. B. Say, and Murray N. Rothbard, have proposed that the troy ounce replace all national currencies (such as the dollar, the franc, the mark) as the national unit of account. J. B. Say, though he did not comment specifically on the 100 percent proposals, favored the use of bullion weights rather than names for currencies: "Why give a denomination to this fixed, imaginary value, which money can never possess? For what is a dollar, a ducat, a florin, a pound sterling, or a franc; what, but a certain weight of gold or silver of a certain established standard of quality? And, if this be all, why give these respective portions of bullion any other name, than the natural one of their weight and quality?"

> Five *grammes* of silver, says the law, shall be equivalent to a *franc*; which is just as much as to say, 5 *grammes* of silver. For the only idea presented to the mind by the word *franc* is the 5 *grammes* of silver it contains. Do wheat, chocolate, or wax, change their name by the mere act of apportioning their weight? A pound weight of bread, chocolate, or of wax candles, is still called a pound weight of bread, chocolate, or wax candles. Why, then, should not a piece of silver, weighing 5 *grammes*, go by its natural appellation? Why not call it simply 5 *grammes* of silver?[2]

---

2. J. B. Say, *A Treatise on Political Economy, or the Production, Distribution and Consumption of Wealth* (Philadelphia, Pa.: Claxton, Remsen, & Haffenlfinger, 1880), p. 256.

In summary, Say considered this change very practical, demonstrating the barter involved in all market exchanges, and this plan would also expose the ". . . system replete with fraud, injustice, and robbery, and moreover so complicated. . . ."[3]

Nearly half a century later, Charles H. Carroll, "A Merchant of Massachusetts," attacked the confusing nature of the national currency system, and called for the elimination of the dollar as the monetary unit in the U.S., to be replaced by the troy ounce. Carroll maintained that false monetary ideas have originated from separation of the monetary unit from the monetary substance.[4]

Murray Rothbard states that in "a purely free market, gold would simply be exchanged directly as 'grams,' grains, or ounces, and such confusing names as dollars, francs, etc. would be superfluous."[5] Elsewhere, he comments:

> Commodities on the market exchanged by their unit weights, and gold and silver were no exceptions. When someone sold copper to buy gold and then to buy butter, he sold *pounds* of copper for *ounces* or *grams* of gold to buy pounds of butter. On the free market, therefore, the monetary unit—the units of the nation's accounts—naturally emerges as the unit of weight of the money commodity, for example, the silver ounce, or the gold gram.[6]

Parallel Standards vs. Bimetallism

Throughout monetary history, gold has become the supreme unit of account, but silver has always been a leading commodity money, and in some countries has been chosen over gold. The existence of two or more commodity monies raises the age-old question of how they should be valued in the monetary system. Should silver be tied to or fixed in exchange for gold, or should it be allowed to fluctuate according to market forces of supply and demand?

---

3. Ibid., p. 257.
4. Charles H. Carroll, *Organization of Debt*, p. xiii.
5. Murray Rothbard, *What Has Government Done to Our Money?* (Santa Ana, Calif.: Rampart College, 1974), p. 7.
6. Murray Rothbard, *Case for the 100 Percent*, p. 6.

Most of the bullion supporters have favored parallel gold and silver standards rather than bimetallism, where an exchange rate between the two metals is arbitrarily fixed. Parallel standards would mean freely fluctuating exchange rates between gold and silver. William Brough, writing before the turn of the century, called this system, "Free Metallism," and said that "No government has ever yet succeeded in holding silver and gold at any fixed ratio of value; the efforts made to accomplish this object have only tended to disturb natural values, to impair the efficiency of money, and to retard industrial progress." Gold and silver should be allowed to "circulate independently" so that "the two metals can be brought into efficient monetary service at the same time in one country." Brough also stated that other metals could come into being as money, if they serve an economic function.[7]

J. B. Say agreed with this view, saying that "it is impossible in practice to assign any fixed ratio of exchangeable value to commodities whose ratio is forever fluctuating, and, therefore, that gold and silver must be left to find their own mutual level, in the transactions in which mankind may think proper to employ them."[8] Say also said that the same principles apply to silver and copper.

Depending on the country or community, one or the other money (gold or silver) would serve as their unit of account, and the price of the other metal would be quoted in terms of the unit of account. Historically, silver has usually been quoted in terms of gold, but note that "from 1664 down to 1717, the relation of gold to silver was not fixed by authority, and, silver being then the only legal tender, the value of gold coins fluctuated according to the fluctuations in the relative worth of the metals in the market."[9] In the bullion certificate program outlined by Isaiah W. Sylvester, gold bullion would serve as the primary unit of account, but silver

---

7. William Brough, *The Natural Law of Money* (New York: G. P. Putnam's Sons, 1894) , pp. 134-39.

8. J. B. Say, *Treatise*, p. 255. Further discussion of a parallel standard can be found in Jevons, *Money and the Mechanism*, p. 94.

9. F. A. Walker, *Money*, p. 224.

bars would be legal tender also, and would be priced in terms of gold bars.[10]

In the 1830s, William Gouge and Condy Raguet both thought that the U.S. should adopt a silver dollar standard, with gold being expressed in terms of silver dollars.[11]

Bimetallism, the system of legislative fixing of the exchange rate between gold and silver, has been generally regarded as a form of price control, and therefore undesirable from a free market point of view.[12] Brough blames this "artificial obstruction" in bimetallism on the government for the creation of Gresham's Law, which states that "bad money drives out good."[13] Gresham's Law would not occur on the free market, according to Brough: "The more efficient money will always drive from circulation the less efficient if the individuals who handle money are left free to act in their own interest. It is only when bad money is endorsed by the State with the property of legal tender that it can drive good money from circulation."[14] Later, writers such as Ludwig von Mises show that Gresham's Law is caused by government intervention rather than a characteristic of the free market. The government's artificial fixing of the exchange rates between gold and silver creates a shortage of the artificially *undervalued* money ("good money") and a surplus of the *overvalued* money ("bad money"). Mises states:

> As two previous metals were used side by side as money, authorities naively believed that it was their task to unify the currency system by decreeing a rigid exchange ratio between gold and silver. The bimetallic system proved a complete failure. It did not

---

10. Isaiah W. Sylvester, *Bullion Certificates*.
11. Joseph Dorfman, *Economic Mind*, p. 610.
12. J. B. Say, *Treatise*, p. 254.
13. Gresham's Law is named after Sir Thomas Gresham, founder of the English Royal Exchange in the 16th Century during the reign of Queen Elizabeth. According to Gresham's Law, if the government sets the exchange value between two metals, the overvalued ("bad") metal will circulate while the undervalued ("good") metal will be hoarded.
14. William Brough, *Open Mints and Free Banking* (New York: Putnam, 1898), pp. 35-36. See also Brough, *Natural Law of Money*, p. 136.

> bring about bimetallism, but an alternating standard. That metal which, compared with the instantaneous state of the fluctuating market exchange rate between gold and silver, was overvalued in the legally fixed ratio, predominated in domestic circulation, while the other metal disappeared. Finally the governments abandoned their vain attempts and acquiesced in monometallism.[15]

Luigi Einaudi explains how bimetallism could work in the short run, when the fixed exchange rate approximates the market price. But this could not last forever. The central bank or mint could postpone a breakdown in bimetallism by absorbing most of the gold or silver bullion offered on the market at the fixed price, as long as the differential between the legal rate and the market price was not substantial. Otherwise, such a policy would lead to an "alternating monometallic standard," as referred to by Mises. Einaudi also mentions the use of two stopgap measures—substantial "seigniorage" charges, or occasionally adjusting the legal ratio to approximate the market price.[16]

Coinage

The basic form of processed gold or silver is bullion, and these ingots or bars of bullion would be used for very large transactions and would serve as the basis for the monetary unit of account under a pure specie standard. Bullion bars or wafers are not practical for small transactions, however, and therefore various gold and silver coins would be used for that purpose.

How should coins be certified? Should they circulate by weight or tale? Should private coinage be allowed? What is the role of government in minting coins? Should coins be legal tender? Who should bear the costs of minting? What should be the role of token coins? These are serious questions which must be raised under any monetary standard.

---

15. Ludwig von Mises, *Human Action* (Chicago, Ill.: Regnery, 1963), p. 781.

16. Luigi Einaudi, "The Theory of Imaginary Money from Charlemagne to the French Revolution," in Lane and Riemersma, *Enterprise*, pp. 239-41.

Circulation by Weight or Tale?

Originally, the first coins circulated by weight only. Stamping of ingots involved the certifying of quality or fineness only, but not the weight.[17] Currency did not circulate by tale or number until the weights of coins were fairly uniform. Since then publicly certified coins have so commonly circulated by tale that Jevons, for example, defines coins as "ingots of which the weight and fineness are certified by the integrity of designs impressed upon the surfaces of the metal."[18]

Certifying coins by weight and fineness is not without major problems, however. William Brough notes that Gresham's Law would never have been heard of had coin passed by weight only, because in that case the recipient would have taken the coin only at the market value of the precious metal it contained."[19] Gresham's Law is caused in this case by the wear of coins, and the certification of weight makes them equal to newly minted full-bodied coins. Over time, this has disastrous effects. Rothbard states:

> Suppose, for example, there are 1-ounce gold coins in circulation. After a few years of wear-and-tear, let us say that some coins weigh only .9 oz. Obviously, on the free market, the worn coins would circulate at only 90 percent of the value of the full-bodied coins, and the nominal face-value of the former would have to be repudiated. If anything, it will be the "bad" coins that will be driven from the market. But suppose the government decrees that everyone must treat the worn coins as equal to new, fresh coins, and must accept them equally in payment of debts. What has the government really done? It has imposed *price control* by coercion on the "exchange rate" between the two types of coins. By insisting on a par-ratio when the worn coins should exchange at a 10 percent discount, it artificially *overvalues* the worn coins and

---

17. Arthur R. Burns, *Money and Monetary Policy*, p. 59. Also, Adam Smith, *Wealth of Nations*, p. 25; Mises, *Theory of Money and Credit*, p. 72.

18. W. S. Jevons, *Money and Mechanisms*, p. 56.

19. William Brough, *Natural Law of Money*, p.23.

> *undervalues* new coins. Consequently, everyone will circulate worn coins, and hoard or export the new.[20]

From the above statement, Rothbard obviously favors circulation of coins by weight, not by tale. However, while there may be major problems with government-certified coins by weight, there are also problems of convenience associated with coins circulating by weight only. J. B. Say, for example, was highly critical of coins circulating by weight: "What inconvenience must ensue were it necessary to be always provided with scales to weigh the money paid or received; and what infinite blunders and disputes must arise from awkwardness or defective implements."[21]

Say also mentioned the difficulties of detecting counterfeiting. Carl Menger points out several "chief defects" in this system, and argues that the exactness of weights requires "labor, loss of time, and precision instruments . . ."[22] Adam Smith brings up the "trouble" and "inconvenience" of weighing and assaying gold and silver, which has led to the "grossest frauds and impositions." Consequently, "To prevent such abuses, to facilitate exchanges, and thereby to encourage all sorts of industry and commerce, it has been found necessary, in all countries that have made any considerable advances towards improvements, to affix a public stamp (stating both fineness and weight) upon certain quantities of such particular metals."[23]

There may be several market solutions to this problem of wear on coins and Gresham's Law. Rothbard suggests, for example, that "To meet the problem of wear-and-tear, private coiners might either set a time limit on their stamped guarantees of weight, or agree to recoin anew, either at the original or at the lower weight."[24]

Despite the disadvantages of coins circulating by weight and

---

20. Murray Rothbard, *What has Government Done*, pp. 10-11. See also Menger, *Principles*, p. 284.
21. J. B. Say, *Treatise*, p. 229.
22. Carl Menger, *Principles*, pp. 280-281.
23. Adam Smith, *Wealth of Nations*, pp. 24-25.
24. Murray Rothbard, *What Has Government Done*, p. 9n.

tale, most partisans to hard money support some form of state intervention in the minting of coins. As Mises states, ". . . the whole aim and intent of State intervention in the monetary sphere is simply to release individuals from the necessity of testing the weight and fineness of the gold they receive, a task which can only be undertaken by experts and which involves very elaborate precautionary measures."[25]

Token Coins

One of the most important measures taken by governments has been the introduction of token coins, or coins whose nominal value is far greater than their metallic value. Token coins have generally been the method by which governments and kings have debased the national currency, and consequently the use of token coins has always been greeted with great suspicion by hard money adherents.

However, Menger, Jevons and others have suggested that token coins can serve the useful purpose of being "representative money," that is, claims to a specified amount of gold or silver at the mint, much in the same way that paper notes or certificates represent claims for a specified quantity of specie. According to Menger, this would alleviate the major problem of Gresham's Law taking effect when governments guarantee the weight of coins.[26] It would also permit private mints to circulate token coins under the same claim, thus eliminating the need for constant weighing. The constant wear and tear on the token coin would not result in the depreciation of the coin's value. They could be exchanged at any time for either new token coins or the actual metal it represents.

Jevons argues that originally "representative money" such as token coins and bank deposits were created in large part to avoid the high costs of weighing and assaying individual coins from foreign lands. Merchants in Italy would receive all kinds of depreci-

---

25. Ludwig von Mises, *Theory of Money and Credit*, pp. 66-67.
26. Carl Menger, *Principles*, p. 284.

ated, clipped and foreign coins, and deposit them in a bank where they were assayed and weighed once and for all, and placed at the credit of the merchant.[27] Thus, token coins did not serve simply as a way to debase the currency, but were essentially a market solution to the problems of weighing, assaying, and depreciation of coins.

The use of token coins as strictly "representative money" does not solve this market problem entirely, however, according to critics. Counterfeiting may become a problem when token coins are used extensively in place of full-bodied, highly valuable gold or silver coins. Feaveryear comments on this potentially grave problem:

> Here we have a picture of the difficulty which persisted almost down to modern times. So long as the coins contained much less than their face value of metal, there was a great temptation to copy them. The technique of coining was still not sufficiently good to give to the money a stamp which it was beyond the skill of the forger to imitate even upon a scale large enough to make it worth while in cases of halfpennies and farthings, and the machinery for the detection of crime was bad. Consequently in a few years the counterfeiters created a glut however much the official coins might be restricted, and any attempt to regulate the circulation to the public need by taking back surplus coins merely put a premium upon counterfeiting.[28]

As a result, both the cost of minting token representative coins and the cost of dealing with additional counterfeiting must be weighed against the benefits of token coinage.

The Cost of Minting

Another major question has been whether the mint should charge for the costs of minting new coins, known technically as "brassage." The mint has essentially three choices: to charge a fee

---

27. W. S. Jevons, *Money and Mechanisms*, pp. 195-196. See *Supra*, p. 18, for quote.

28. A. E. Feaveryear, *Pound Sterling*, p. 158.

greater than costs (traditionally known as "seigniorage"), or a price just covering costs ("brassage"), or to supply coins free of charge. Seigniorage is the custom of charging far in excess of the actual costs of coinage for political reasons and for revenue purposes, and has little economic justification except to keep coins from being exported. It does raise the spectre of counterfeiting, however.[29]

Rothbard is critical of both seigniorage and gratuitous coinage. "Seigniorage was a monopoly price, and it imposed a special burden on the conversion of bullion to coin; gratuitous coinage, on the other hand, overstimulated the manufacture of coins from bullion, and forced the general taxpayer to pay for minting services used by others."[30]

J. B. Say, noting that the coining of money provides a service to its users, concludes that coins should sell at a premium, to be charged by the mint. According to Say, when the government defrays the cost of coinage, as the British government did in the early 1800s by taxation, coins such as the guineas tend to become underpriced and exported; this is because at the same price the coins provide greater value, since assaying and weighing have already been done.[31] Say, however, believed that the community at large should pay for the ordinary wear and tear of legal tender coins.[32]

Private Coinage

Throughout history, and even during the height of the gold standard era, there have been few hard money writers who have publicly supported the idea of private coinage. Adam Smith, a leader of laissez faire economics, still felt that private coinage is

29. F. A. Walker, *Money*, pp. 184-186.

30. Murray Rothbard, *What Has Government Done*, pp. 31-32.

31. J. B. Say, *Treatise*, pp. 229-231.

32. Ibid., p. 265: "I am inclined to think, the loss by wear, and that of the impression, should be borne by the community by large; that is to say, by the public purse: for the whole society derives the benefit of the money; and it is impossible to tax each individual, in the precise proportion of the use he has made of it."

the basis of the "grossest frauds and impositions," and to prevent abuses requires the need for public mints.[33]

J. B. Say, another free trader, stated that "though governments have too often broken faith in this particular, their guarantee is still preferred by the people to that of individuals, both for the sake of uniformity in the coin, and because there would probably be more difficulty in detecting the frauds of private issuers."[34] Jevons rejects private coinage, basing this rejection on his belief that under private industry, "bad money drives out good" (Gresham's Law) and counterfeiting and debasing of the currency would be widespread. He is quick to point out that "No doubt, in times past, kings have been the most notorious false coiners and depreciators of the currency, but there is no danger of the like being done in modern times."[35] And Brough adds, "there is a natural tendency to the depreciation of the metallic currency, which can only be prevented by the constant supervision of the state."[36]

Arthur R. Burns, in his history of money in early times, concludes that "The wide variation in the proportion of gold in the early electrum pieces suggests that the opportunity was seen and exploited by many private coiners, although it is perhaps too sweeping a condemnation to say that 'the system of free private coining became everywhere a system of false coining.'" Burns, for example, notes that in consequence of this weakness and the appearance of counterfeits, "pieces bearing some marks gained more general acceptance than others."[37]

The natural inclination to accept only private minters who had established a good reputation among the people is commented further by Burns: "The seals more frequently met with, and those on which experience taught people to rely, gained special respect, and pieces bearing them became commoner mediums of exchange than pieces with other marks. In some

33. Adam Smith, *Wealth of Nations*, p. 25.
34. J. B. Say, *Treatise*, p. 229.
35. W. S. Jevons, *Money and Mechanism*, pp. 63-64.
36. William Brough, *Natural Law of Money*, p. 15.
37. Arthur R. Burns, *Money and Monetary Policy*, p. 78.

areas, and particularly in Asia Minor and Lydia, it was in fact, the pieces of the most wealthy and powerful merchant that became best known. Where he elected openly to assume political power the issue of money was vested in the tyrant from the beginning, and by the use of his political power to suppress any small competitors that remained, he secured a monopoly of coining."[38]

A group of French supporters of laissez faire have written in favor of private mints. In *Traite d' Economie Politique*, Leroy-Beaulieu suggests that due to public abuse of coinage and national currencies, it might be better if private banks of established reputation be permitted to coin money.[39] Another Frenchman, J. E. Horn, argues that firms such as Rothschild in Paris or Baring in London could undertake the stamping of coins and be well accepted by the public.[40]

Professor Milton Friedman has, remarkably, made a similar stand. Friedman argues that although government in the past has certified both weight and fineness, there should be no reason why the market cannot provide this service adequately, borrowing perhaps from the "Good Housekeeping" seal of approval.[41]

Murray Rothbard is one of the staunch advocates of private mints over public mints.

> The pretext for socialization of minting—one which has curiously been accepted by almost every economist—is that private minters would defraud the public on the weight and fineness of coins. This argument rings peculiarly hollow when we consider the long record of governmental debasement of the coinage and of the monetary standard. But apart from this, we certainly know that private enterprise has been able to supply an almost infinite number of goods requiring high precision standards; yet nobody

---

38. Ibid., p. 445.

39. Paul Leroy-Beaulieu, *Traite d' Economie Politique* (Paris, 1910), III, p. 128. See also Charles A. Conant, *The Principles of Money and Banking* (New York: Harper & Bro., 1905), I, pp. 127-28. Conant also reports on private mints in the U.S. and Europe (pp. 129-32).

40. J. E. Horn, *La Liberte des Banques* (1866), referred to in Vera Smith, *Rationale for Central Banking*, pp. 93-94.

41. Milton Friedman, *Monetary Stability*, p. 5.

advocates nationalization of the machine tool industry or the electronics industry in order to safeguard these standards. And no one wants to abolish all contracts because some people might commit fraud in making them. Surely the proper remedy for any fraud is the defense of property rights.[42]

Legal Tender Laws

Legal tender laws, which require the seller to accept legal payment for a debt, are called "superfluous at best, mischievous and a means of arbitrary exchange-rate fixing at worst."[43] William Brough was thoroughly opposed to legal tender laws, which he says makes people distrust government money. He points to the Continental bills as an example. He concludes: "There is no more case for a special law to compel the receiving of money than there is for one to compel the receiving of wheat or of cotton. The common law is as adequate for the enforcement of contracts in the one case as in the other."[44]

Jevons notes how specie was able to obtain universal acceptance without legal tender laws: "The possibility of international currency is proved by the fact that, without any international treaties, the coins of several nations are recognized as legal tender elsewhere," using examples such as the English sovereigns, the napoleon, the ducat of Holland, and the Mexican dollar.[45]

The social philosopher Herbert Spencer takes a laissez faire position on this issue: "For either to forbid the issue or enforce the receipt of certain notes or coin in return for other things is to infringe the right of exchange—is to prevent men making exchanges

42. Murray Rothbard, *Case for 100 Percent*, pp. 12-13. Also, *idem*, *What Has Government Done*, pp. 8-10. Others to support private mints include Herbert Spencer, *Social Statics* (New York: Appleton, 1890), pp. 438-39; Leonard Read, *Government—An Ideal Concept* (Irving-on-Hudson, N.Y.: Foundation for Economic Education, 1954), pp. 82ff; Lysander Spooner, *A Letter to Grover Cleveland* (Boston: Tucker, 1886), p. 79; J. Laurence Laughlin, *A New Exposition of Money, Credit and Prices* (Chicago: University Press, 1931), I, pp. 47-51.

43. Murray Rothbard, *Case for 100 Percent*, p. 16n.

44. William Brough, *Natural Law of Money*, pp. 135, 77.

45. W. S. Jevons, *Money and Mechanism*, p. 168.

which they otherwise would have made, or to oblige them to make exchanges which they otherwise would not have made.[46]

Paper Money Substitutes

Paper money can play a definite, powerful role under the 100 percent specie standard. Although some hard money advocates, such as Thomas Jefferson, at times favored the abolition of paper money entirely because of its "misuse," others have pointed out that the economic advantages of paper money can be had without the disadvantages created through the fractional reserve system. Paper money turns out to be a very cheap and efficient way for the handling and transferring of metallic money. The actual transfer of gold or silver can be an expensive process, especially for large transactions, and consequently the transfer of claims for money proves to be much more convenient and efficient.[47]

A fundamental postulate of the 100 percent specie doctrine is that paper money literally is a warehouse receipt or certificate for the commodity money it represents, just as it was under the scriveners and early goldsmith-bankers. As previously noted, originally goldsmith notes were bailee notes, non-assignable warehouse receipts, or dock warrants.[48] Referred to in legal terms as specific deposit warrants, or documents titles, these warehouse receipts represent claims of ownership.

> Documents of title, such as bills of lading, warehouse receipts, and dock warrants, are symbols of ownership in goods. A bill of lading is "a receipt by the carrier for goods to be shipped, coupled

---

46. Herbert Spencer, *Social Statics*, p. 354.

47. William Brough advanced the advantages of paper money. Cf. *Natural Law of Money*, p. 64. Also Rothbard, *What Has Government Done*, pp. 19-20. Adam Smith recognized these advantages, but thought that they came only through fractional reserves.

48. R. D. Richards, *Banking in England*, pp. 223-25. Jevons, *Money and Mechanism*, p. 197. E. T. Powell, *Evolution of Money Markets*, p. 62ff. J. E. Thorold Rogers, *First Nine Years of the Bank of England* (London, 1887), p. 8, notes that deposit slips in early "banks of deposit" were "of the nature of dock warrants, entitling the holder to claim not only the sum which they expressed, but, theoretically at least, the very coins which were deposited against them."

> with an agreement for their carriage according to the terms expressed in the bill.". . . A warehouse receipt, closely resembling a bill of lading as a document of title, is a written acknowledgement of the receipt of goods, and a contract of storage between the warehouseman and the depositor of goods.[49]

A bailment is defined as "the transfer of personal property to another person with the understanding that the property is to be returned when a certain purpose has been completed. . . . In a sale, we relinquish both title and possession. In a bailment, we merely give up temporarily the possession of the goods."[50]

Concerning the use of specific deposit warrants as money claims, Jevons remarks: "The most satisfactory kind of promissory document . . . is presented by bills of lading, pawn-tickets, dock-warrants, or certificates which establish ownership to a definite object . . . The important point concerning such promissory notes is, that they cannot possibly be issued in excess of the goods actually deposited, unless by distinct fraud. The issuer ought to act purely as a warehouse-keeper and as possession may be claimed at any time, he can never legally allow any object deposited to go out of his safe keeping until it is delivered back in exchange for the promissory note."[51]

Because of the homogeneous nature of money, however, the public is generally uninterested in specific coins or notes. Thus, money claims or certificates can be used far more efficiently and less costly in exchange if they are legally defined as "general deposit warrants," under which "the issuer of a promissory document engages to keep on hand goods exactly equivalent in quantity and quality to what are specified thereon, without taking note of individual parcels."[52] The major drawback to general, as opposed to specific, warrants is that "it will be necessary to present

---

49. William H. Spencer, *A Textbook of Law and Business* (New York: McGraw-Hill, 1938, 2nd ed.), p. 732.

50. Robert O. Sklar and Benjamin W. Palmer, *Business Law* (New York: McGraw-Hill, 1942), p. 361.

51. W. S. Jevons, *Money and Mechanism*, p. 202.

52. Ibid., pp. 202-03.

most or all of the documents in order to disclose default," as Jevons puts it. "The receiver of deposits, finding that a large portion of the deposited commodity always remains on hand, may proceed to use it as trade, only keeping so much as may meet current demands." Thus, it becomes possible to create a "fictitious supply of a commodity."[53] This is precisely what the goldsmith-bankers instigated.

To avoid this problem, Rothbard suggests that the legal system "consider all 'general deposit warrants' (which allow the warehouse to return any homogeneous good to the depositor), as 'specific deposit warrants,' which, like bills of lading, pawn tickets, dock warrants, etc., establish ownership to certain specific earmarked objects. For, in the case of a general deposit warrant, the warehouse is tempted to treat the goods as its own property, instead of being the property of its customers. This is precisely what the banks have been doing."[54]

The same principle applies to the use of checks in redeeming money on deposit. Like token coins and banknotes, checks and deposits are, from an economic point of view, essentially claims to the ownership of money or specie and are transferred similarly as money substitutes.[55]

The Role of Banking

The structure of banking would be changed radically under a pure 100 percent specie standard. The 100 percent reserve system would require that "any institution which accepts deposits payable on demand or transferable by check to have one dollar in high-powered money for every dollar in deposit liabilities (whether nominally demand or time deposits)."[56]

Irving Fisher, in explaining a 100 percent fiduciary standard

53. Ibid., pp. 204-05.

54. Murray Rothbard, *What Has Government Done*, p. 24n.

55. Ibid., p. 21.

56. Milton Friedman, *Monetary Stability*, p. 69. Although Friedman here refers to a fiduciary dollar system, the 100 percent specie standard would require all dollars to be backed by 100 percent gold or silver.

(but which equally applies to a pure commodity standard), elucidates how the system would work. All banks would be required to maintain 100 percent reserves so that "demand deposits would literally be deposits, consisting of cash held in trust for the depositor. . . . The checking deposit department of the bank would become a mere storage warehouse for bearer money belonging to its depositors. . . .[57] Thus, "The proposal to require 100% reserves for deposits involves applying the same policy to deposits that we have applied to currency."[58]

Jevons refers to this system as a "simple deposit" method of currency: "The amount of such a currency will vary exactly like that of a metallic currency, and there can be no fear of paper replacing specie, and driving it out of the country, because the specie must be in the vaults of the issuing bank before the notes are issued."[59]

Legal Applications of 100 Percent Proposal

The institution of 100 percent banking would require a fundamental transformation in the legal framework of present-day banking. As discussed earlier since the beginning of fractional reserve banking, the banker has been legally in the position of a debtor, not a bailee or warehouse custodian of customers' accounts. The present arrangement is such that, in reality, when money is deposited, it actually becomes the property of the bank, not the depositor's. In essence, the effect of a sale of property has taken place. In return, the depositor receives the right to demand an equivalent amount of cash.[60] Under the present system,

---

57. Irving Fisher, *100% Money*, p. 10.
58. Milton Friedman, *Monetary Stability*, p. 67.
59. W. S. Jevons, *Money and Mechanism*, pp. 216-217.
60. Charles F. Dunbar, *Theory and History of Banking* (New York: Putnam, 1901), pp. 14-15. See also Powell, *Money Market*, pp. 62-73. Strangely enough, Dunbar contends that banking consists solely in the lending process and that the safekeeping role is not actually a banking function. "It is true that money may be left as a 'special deposit' with a bank, just as plate, jewels, or other valuables may be, in which case, the identical money deposited is to be returned, and the bank consequently does not acquire the property in the thing deposited, but is merely entrusted with its temporary custody. This, however, is not a banking operation, and the deposit in this case is made with the bank, not because it is a bank, but because it owns a strong vault."

"While the average depositor imagines he has 'cash in the bank,' bankers know that this 'cash' is really only 'credit,' that is, a debt of the bank to the depositor."[61]

A radical change would therefore be required so that demand deposits would be legally regarded as deposits of ownership, not simply credit. In this vein, Rothbard advocates that "the law be changed to treat banknotes and deposits as what they are in economic and social fact: claims, warehouse receipts to standard money—in short, that the note- and deposit-holders be recognized as owners-in-law of the gold (or, under a fiat standard, of the paper) in the bank's vaults. Now treated in law as a debt, a deposit or note should be considered as evidence of a bailment. In relation to general legal principles this would not be a radical change, since warehouse receipts are treated as bailments now. Banks would simply be treated as money warehouses in relation to their notes and deposits."[62] In addition, banknotes would be treated as "money certificates," or claims to a specified amount of money held by the bank.[63]

How Banking Would Operate Under the 100 Percent Rule

The essence of the 100 percent program is "to make money independent of loans; that is, to divorce the process of creating and destroying money from the business of banking," as Irving Fisher puts it. "What makes the trouble is the fact that the bank (under a fractional reserve system) lends not money but merely a promise to furnish money on demand—money it does not possess."[64] Fisher elaborates by saying that the 100 percent rule is:

> A return from the present extraordinary and ruinous system of lending the same money 8 or 10 times over, to the conservative

---

61. Irving Fisher, *100% Money*, p. 54.

62. Murray Rothbard, *Case for 100 Percent*, pp. 23-24.

63. Ludwig von Mises, *Human Action*, p. 433: "If the debtor—the government or a bank—keeps against the whole amount of money-substitutes a 100% reserve of money proper, we call the money-substitute a *money-certificate.*"

64. Irving Fisher, *100% Money*, pp. xvii, 8.

safety-deposit system of the old goldsmiths, before they began lending out improperly what was entrusted to them for safekeeping. It was this abuse of trust which, after being accepted as standard practice, evolved into modern deposit banking. From the standpoint of public trust it is still an abuse, no longer an abuse of trust but an abuse of the loan and deposit functions.[65]

In his work, *A Program for Monetary Stability*, Friedman outlines "How 100% Reserves Would Work":

> The effect of this proposal would be to require our present commercial banks to divide themselves into two separate institutions. One would be a pure depository institution, a literal warehouse for money. It would accept deposits payable on demand or transferable by check. For every dollar of deposit liabilities, it would be required to have a dollar of high-powered money among its assets in the form, say, either of Federal Reserve notes or Federal Reserve deposits. This institution would have no funds, except the capital of its proprietors, which it could lend on the market. An increase in deposits would not provide it with funds to lend since it would be required to increase its assets in the form of high-powered money dollar for dollar. The other institution that would be formed would be an investment trust or brokerage firm. It would acquire capital by selling shares or debentures and would use the capital to make loans or acquire investments.[66]

Isolating the deposit function of banks would of course necessitate the charging of a fee for the service of safekeeping of funds and the checking privilege. On this score, Rothbard comments on warehouses in general:

> Their profits are earned from service charges to their customers. The banks can charge for their services in the same way. If it is objected that customers will not pay the high service charges, then this means that the banks' services are not in very great demand, and the use of their services will fall to the levels that consumers find worthwhile.[67]

---

65. Ibid., pp. 18-19.
66. Milton Friedman, *Monetary Stability*, pp. 69-70.
67. Murray Rothbard, *What Has Government Done*, p. 22. See also Fisher, *100% Money*, p. 10.

Loans Under the 100 Percent Rule

Under a pure specie standard, banks would no longer be able to use demand deposits as a source of lending. This does not mean, however, that banks would be legally excluded from all lending activities. On the contrary, as an entirely separate function, banks would be able to obtain moneys for lending purposes from the following main sources: (1) their own capital, (2) bona fide savings accounts, with varying degrees of maturation, and (3) money earned from maturing loans.[68] On this subject, Mises comments: "The issue of money-certificates does not increase the funds which the bank can employ in the conduct of its lending business. A bank which does not issue fiduciary media can only grant commodity credit, i.e., it can only lend its own funds and the amount of money which its customers have entrusted to it."[69]

Rothbard elaborates on the existence and use of credit under a 100 percent standard. Banks, he notes, "may still lend their own saved funds (capital stock and accumulated surplus) or they may borrow funds from individuals and relend them to business firms, earning the interest differential. Borrowing money (e.g., floating a bond) is a credit transaction; an individual exchanges his present money for a bond—a claim on future money. The borrowing banks pay him interest for this loan and in turn exchanges the money thus gathered for promises by business borrowers to pay money in the future. This is a further credit transaction, in this case the bank acting as the lender and businesses as the borrowers. The bank's income is the interest differential between the two types of credit transactions; the payment is for the services of the bank as an intermediary, channeling the savings of the public into investment. There is, furthermore, no particular reason why the short-term, more than any other, credit market should be subsidized by money creation."[70]

---

68. Irving Fisher, *100% Money*, p. 17.

69. Ludwig von Mises, *Human Action*, p. 433.

70. Murray Rothbard, *Man, Economy and State: A Treatise on Economic Principles* (Los Angeles, Calif.: Nash Publishing, 1970), p. 708. See also Rothbard, *The Mystery of Banking*, pp. 77-85. "Loan banking is a productive, noninflationary institution." (p. 81).

Thus, in conclusion, a banker becomes a "middleman," according to William Brough, where "he would himself become the borrower from those who wished to lend, and the lender to those who wished to borrow," the differential in interest rates being the banker's profit.[71]

Savings Accounts and Time Deposits

The absolute 100 percent reserve restrictions would not apply to bona fide credit transactions, which of course the banks could compete in as would any other financial institution. As Charles Carroll writes, 100 percent reserves of specie would be required on all "demand liabilities," but there would be no control of savings accounts.[72] Undoubtedly, bank regulators would pay special attention to the activity of savings accounts. So-called "time deposits" which offer withdrawal on demand would be treated in the same manner as regular demand deposits or checking accounts, requiring 100 percent reserves.

Under bona fide savings accounts, the debtor-creditor relationship would continue. The customer would not be making a "deposit," but rather a "loan," of varying maturity. He could not request or demand an immediate withdrawal of his funds, nor could he liquidate the loan by check. "The customer would have to understand he could not demand his money at any time and be paid in full. He would have to understand that he is taking a credit risk and that his money will be re-loaned through proper channels, of course, but in such a way that he cannot, by demanding his money, force the savings banker into a drastic liquidation of his loans."[73]

---

71. William Brough, *Law of Money,* p. 62.

72. Charles H. Carroll, "Mr. Lowell vs. Mr. Cooper on Banking and Currency," and "Currency of the United States," *Organization of Debt*. Also, Mints, *History of Banking Theory,* p. 156.

73. Letter by two bankers, F. D. von Wendegger and W. L. Gregory of the Plaza Bank of St. Louis, quoted in Fisher, *100% Money,* pp. 167-68.

Summary

In advocating the uninhibited, complete specie standard, proponents basically view their task as one of eliminating as much as possible the sources of instability within the monetary system. These areas of instability might include rapid inflation, speculative booms followed by destructive depressions, balance of payment crises, the frequent disappearance or export of domestic gold or silver coins, the debasing of national currencies, and so forth.

Although hard money adherents envision an important role for government to play in the monetary sphere (such as the enforcement of contracts, punishment of fraudulent banking activities, restrictions on reserve requirements), that role is often severely limited. In fact, most would regard government as the chief source of instability in the monetary and banking world. As an alternative, "free market" solutions are most often advocated as a way to solve these government-created problems.

The 100 percent advocates, for example, contend that bimetallism, a common monetary program in past centuries where the rate of exchange between gold and silver is artificially set by government edict, is inherently unstable and the source of Gresham's Law, driving from circulation the undervalued currency in favor of the overvalued currency. As an alternative, a parallel monetary standard, where market forces are permitted to determine the exchange rate between gold and silver, is opted for as a way of restoring financial stability.

In a similar manner, bullion advocates are highly critical of seigniorage, a practice which is considered a burdensome tax on the public, and gratuitous coinage, a practice which can lead to the exportation of domestic currency. The "market" fee of brassage is often recommended as an appropriate alternative.

Coin circulation by weight vs. tale is a more complicated issue, however, since both the market and government solutions seem to have significant drawbacks which can either be cumbersome and open to widespread abuse or create again the ill-effects of Gresham's Law ("bad money drives out the good"). The use of token coins is favorably considered as at least a temporary expedient in solving this difficult problem.

In dealing with the monumental problems of inflation, foreign exchange crises, and the business cycle, which is often considered as the fault of government officials, hard money proponents view the 100 percent specie standard as a relatively ideal reform measure. By requiring financial institutions in custody of the public's funds to maintain 100 percent reserves against demand deposits, advocates hope to abate the menace of monetary instability.

Accordingly, it would seemingly eliminate the discretionary power of the government to debase the currency, since the fiscal agent would be limited in obtaining additional funds from either borrowing or taxation. It could not obtain these additional funds through monetary inflation or the debasement of the currency since fractional reserve banking would not be permitted nor would the government be allowed to print more notes than they had precious metal to back up. Moreover, banks would no longer be a source of economic instability and excess speculation by reducing their reserves to dangerously low levels, thus raising the chances of a bank run and a loss in the public's confidence, which would result in panic and economic ruin for many.

According to adherents, these restrictions would not be overly burdensome. Banks would still be allowed to participate in lending activities and to serve as financial intermediaries, but they could not make use of the customer's demand deposits for lending purposes.

4

Economic Issues of the Pure Specie Framework

In advocating the ultra-hard money stance of the 100 percent specie monetary system, proponents aim to achieve a monetary framework consistent with the free market and property rights in addition to establishing a stable groundwork for economic and banking systems. They have been acutely aware and critical of present banking standards and practices. Their hope is perhaps best expressed in the words of Vera C. Smith: "How to discover a banking system which will not be the cause of catastrophic disturbances, which is least likely itself to introduce oscillations and most likely to make the correct adjustments to counteract changes from the side of the public, is the most acute unsettled economic problem of our day."[1]

Advantages of a Pure Specie Standard

Hard money advocates view their monetary program as an all-encompassing solution to a plethora of economic ills. It is regarded as a system consistent with the property rights of citizens, relatively stable without major cyclical effects, independent of government manipulation, and devoid of inflationary fiduciary issue, currency debasement, international crises and long-term balance of payments deficits.

1. Vera C. Smith, *Central Banking*, p. 171.

Property Rights and Freedom

Under a pure commodity-money standard, the monetary unit of account is to be chosen by the voluntary exchanges between individuals. Historically, this has meant the precious metals, chiefly gold and silver. Under a program of extreme laissez faire, as proposed by Rothbard and others, individuals would have the right to mint their own gold and silver coins, and to compete with others to meet the needs and desires of consumers in their financial needs. In any case, "Money can only be obtained by purchasing it with one's goods and services," except for miners of gold and silver, who would need to invest resources in producing specie.

Accordingly, the 100 percent specie system eliminates "the uneconomic and immoral practice of people acquiring money at the expense of the producer," an alleged characteristic of fractional reserve banking.[2] In the banking sphere, the full property rights of the depositor are upheld, and bankers are responsible for the safekeeping of depositors' funds. Use of these funds for other purposes such as lending would be regarded as a form of fraud or even embezzlement.

An Independent Monetary Authority

The 100 percent specie standard would eliminate the discretionary power of government to directly manipulate the stock of money (it could indirectly manipulate it through subsidies of the production of specie, but this might be expensive). This was one of the primary aims of the Currency Principle and the Peel Act of 1844. "It renders the determination of the monetary unit's purchasing power independent of the policies of governments and political parties," states Mises.[3] Neither government nor banks could increase or decrease the money supply through lending or open-market operations.

Under the 100 percent commodity plan, "The amount of the commodity in use as money would depend on its cost of produc-

---

2. Murray Rothbard, *The Case for 100 Percent*, pp. 6, 38.
3. Ludwig von Mises, *Theory of Money and Credit*, p. 416.

tion relative to other goods, and on the fraction of their wealth people want to hold in the form of money; additions to the stock of money could come from production by private enterprise; changes in the rate of production would reflect changes in the relative value placed on the monetary commodity and other goods or in the relative costs of producing the one and the other."[4]

Economic and Banking Stability

A host of free market economists have emphasized the stable nature of gold and silver as real money. Adam Smith, for example, writes that "The price of those metals, indeed, is not altogether exempted from variation, but the changes to which it is liable are generally slow, gradual, and uniform."[5]

A century later, F. A. Walker argues that:

> The precious metals derive a remarkable degree of durability, from which it results that great changes in the amount of the current production have only a slight effect upon the total volume in the possession of mankind . . . the precious metals derive from their slow consumption in use and their absolute imperishableness in store, a stability which no other important article of commerce attains. From year to year these metals hold their way with great steadiness, while cotton, corn, coal, and most of the necessaries of life fluctuate from month to month, often within a wide range of prices.[6]

Harrison H. Brace explains in further detail the reason for this long-term stability:

> The supply of gold consists primarily of all the mass of the precious metal which has been stored up during the world's previous history. When there is a new influx from the mines, it merely augments the ancient supply, which has been continually added to from the earliest times. Each addition to the supply, however, after it has had its price effect, tends to make the value more stable as it takes its place in the permanent stock. And each sub-

4. Milton Friedman, *Monetary Stability*, pp. 4-5.
5. Adam Smith, *Wealth of Nations*, p. 405.
6. F. A. Walker, *Money*, pp. 43, 158.

> sequent increment of a given amount is less and less percentage of it, so, in the latter part of a great influx of gold, the effects of additions grow smaller and smaller.[7]

To demonstrate how gold functions as an extremely "hard" currency, consider the following example: Suppose there exists approximately 100,000 metric tons in total above-ground supplies in Year 1, and that current output is 1,000 fine tons. The annual growth rate is 1 percent. Now assume that gold production increases by 50 percent to 1,500 tons in Year 2. What is the annual increase in world gold supplies in Year 2? The total gold stock at the beginning of Year 2 is 101,000 tons. The annual growth rate has risen to only 1.48 percent. Look at it another way: In order for the total amount of gold to expand by 4 percent in Year 2, mining companies would have to increase output by 4,000 tons, a 300 percent increase in one year!

Gold's Backward-Bending Supply Curve

Another reason why gold is considered a "hard money" system is its so-called "backward-bending" or "backward-rising" supply curve. Because of this extraordinary phenomenon, gold mining companies are not very responsive in the short run to increases in the demand for gold. Historically, the supply response to higher profitability in gold mining is quite long term. As Jurg Niehans explains, "Since the annual flow of new gold typically is only a fraction of the stock of monetary gold, even a modest increase in the stock demand for money may require many years of temporary above-equilibrium production of gold to be satisfied . . . While gold discoveries will certainly tend to push prices up, it would be a coincidence if the money supply and commodity prices moved up in proportion."[8]

The mining industry has never been very sensitive to business conditions on a short-term basis. In fact, when gold becomes more valuable (either through a rise in the price of gold, or a

7. Brace, *Gold Production and Future Prices* (New York: Bankers Publishing Co., 1910), pp. 112-13.

8. Jurg Niehans, *The Theory of Money* (Baltimore, Maryland: The Johns Hopkins University Press, 1978), pp. 146-47.

decline in prices in general), there is a tendency for mining companies to *reduce* gold output temporarily as miners shift operations toward deeper shafts and less rich ore bodies that might have previously been cost-prohibitive. This may explain why the inflationary 1970s resulted in a short-term reduction in gold output, but eventually led to greater production in the 1980s.[9]

This so-called "backward-rising" supply curve for gold is not really perverse, as some economists have suggested. It reflects the important distinction between the short run and the long run in the mining industry. If the real price of gold is perceived to have risen permanently, the mining industry tends to cut back on *current* output in order to devote more resources to digging deeper and expanding exploration plans in an effort to maximize profits in the long run. The mining industry's approach is remarkably similar to the attitude of savers: temporarily reduce current consumption in order to save and invest, earn a return, and consequently increase consumption in the future. The ultimate effect of this "backward-bending" supply curve is to maximize long-term profits.

Rothbard concludes: "Since the demand for gold and silver was high, and since their supply was low in relation to the demand, the value of each unit in terms of other goods was high—a most useful attribute of money. This scarcity, combined with great durability, meant that the annual fluctuations of supply were necessarily small—another useful feature of a money commodity.[10]

On the subject of gold production and stability, Mises comments that the gold standard "does not lay the prices of commodities open to violent and sudden change from the monetary side. The biggest variations in the value of money that we have experienced during the last century have not originated in the circumstances of gold production, but in the policies of governments and banks-of-issue."[11] Friedman notes the benefits of a 100 percent specie standard in this regard: "Large changes in the stock of money would be unlikely to occur over short periods, hence such

---

9. For a discussion of the "backward-rising supply curve," see Roy Jastram, *The Golden Constant* (New York: Wiley & Sons, 1977), pp. 186-87.

10. Murray Rothbard, *Case for 100 Percent*, p. 6.

11. Ludwig von Mises, *Theory of Money and Credit*, p. 17.

a standard would provide a reasonably stable monetary framework and would not itself be a source of short-run instability."[12]

No Monetary Deflation

One of the most important distinctions of a pure gold standard is that a monetary deflation is virtually impossible. The world supply of gold and hard monetary reserves is always increasing. It is, in fact, inconceivable that a monetary collapse could occur under 100 percent reserves, as happened in 1929-32. During the Great Depression of the 1930s, the money stock fell by one third.[13] Admittedly, this monetary deflation occurred when the United States was on a gold standard, but it was a fractional reserve-based gold standard. Under a pure gold standard, banks would be required to maintain a 100 percent reserve, which would calm the fears the public might have regarding the solvency of banks. Why would panicky depositors want to withdraw their money when the total amount owned is stored safely in the bank's vaults? And even if they did withdraw their funds, the total amount of money would remain unchanged. Under a fractional reserve system, converting deposits to cash can sharply curtail the money supply, but under 100 percent backing, it can have no such effect. Thus, bank runs would have no impact on the supply of money. Moreover, the government could not blunder in reducing the money supply because the monetary stock would consist entirely of gold bullion and coins.

Unlike other metals used for industrial purposes, gold is hardly ever consumed. It simply changes form. The amount of unrecovered gold in industry, or lost in the sea, is relatively small. As Roy Jastram observes, "Gold has two interesting properties: it is cherished and it is indestructible. It is never cast away and it never diminishes, except by outright loss. It can be melted down, but it never changes its chemistry or weight in the process. The ring worn today may contain particles mined in the time of the Pharaohs. In this sense it is also a constant."[14]

---

12. Milton Friedman, *Monetary Stability*, p. 5.
13. Milton Friedman and Anna J. Schwartz, *A Monetary History of the United States, 1867-1960* (Princeton: Princeton University Press, 1963), p. 299.
14. Roy W. Jastram, *The Golden Constant* (New York: John Wiley & Sons, 1977), p. 189.

This fact leads to a significant characteristic of gold as a monetary metal: its supply is always increasing. Throughout history, the total stock of gold has never declined from year to year. The amount of world gold stocks increases every year, depending on annual production. Of course, annual production of the yellow metal rises and falls, but because of gold's relative indestructibility, the total above-ground stocks have never diminished. This constantly increasing level of gold stocks also apparently applies to *monetary* gold stocks held by governments, which involves gold not used for industrial or jewelry purposes. Figure 1 demonstrates the gradual increase in monetary gold levels held by all governments between 1810 and 1934, during which time the Western world was officially on some kind of gold standard. (Note how line "a," "world monetary stock of gold," never declines.) Theoretically, world monetary reserves could decline if the public converted coins or bullion to art or industrial use, but such an event seems unlikely.

Stability in banking is also a major advantage of a pure commodity standard, according to adherents. Under 100 percent reserves, "Shifts between deposits and currency would have no effect on the total stock of money and banks could not alter the ratio of deposits to reserves. The result would be to remove completely any instability in the stock of money arising from these sources. Since all money would in effect become a government obligation, there would be no need for federal insurance of bank deposits."[15] Since the main source of bank failure has been liquidity shortages as a result of a combination of long-term lending and short-term or demand obligations, the 100 percent rule would probably reduce the likelihood of bank failures, and especially runs on the banks by the public.[16]

Monetary Expansion Under Gold

Not only is monetary deflation virtually impossible under gold, but monetary inflation is unlikely to get out of hand. Historically,

---

15. Ibid., p. 69.

16. George S. Tolley, "100 Per Cent Reserve Banking," in Yeager, *Monetary Constitution*, p. 279.

Figure 1

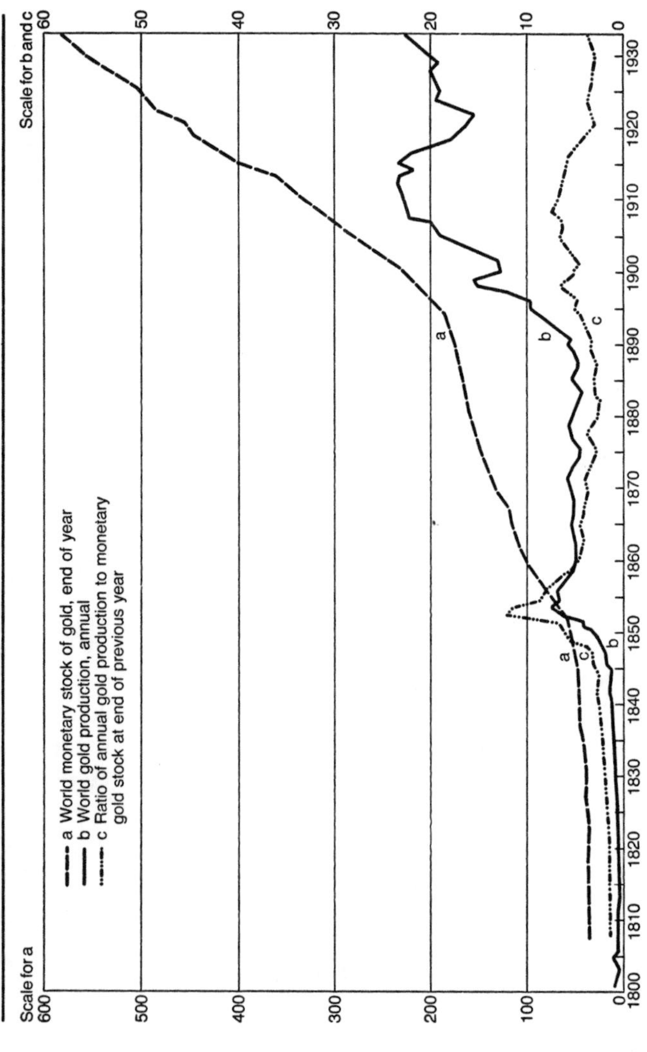
FIGURE 1
World Gold Stock and Gold Production, 1800–1932
Scale for a
Scale for b and c
a World monetary stock of gold, end of year
b World gold production, annual
c Ratio of annual gold production to monetary gold stock at end of previous year
Note: Unit for gold stock and for production is million fine ounces: for the ratio of production to stock, one percent.
Source: Refus S. Tucker, "Gold and the General Price Level," Review of Economic Statistics, July 1934.

monetary expansion under gold has been relatively steady over the long run. Based on several historical studies on world gold production since 1492, mining production never increased the total supply of gold by more than 5 percent in any one year. In fact, except for occasional gold rushes, the total supply of gold has risen steadily at an annual rate of 1-2 percent. Moreover, according to figure 1, total monetary gold also increased steadily between 1821 and 1934. Although this growth rate may not be as constant as the mechanical monetarist rule that Milton Friedman and other monetarists advocate (3-4 percent), it is remarkably stable, and certainly historically more stable than monetary fluctuations under central banks.

While there are no precise figures on the total amount of metal held by governments, individuals and industry, estimates of growth rates in gold supplies can be made based on fairly exact production statistics since the fifteenth century. Based solely on gold output figures since 1492, I estimate that the level of gold holdings increased at an annual rate of less than 1 percent between 1492 and 1840.[17]

The discovery and mining of precious metals in America by the Spanish in the sixteenth century created a massive influx of hard money and a significant rise in prices throughout Europe. According to official records, the Spanish King took in 199.4 tons of gold and 18,246 tons of silver during the sixteenth century.[18] Smuggled gold and silver undoubtedly added substantially to this sum. While this amount may not seem large by today's standards, William Jacob, in his study of the production and consumption of precious metals, estimates that the quantity of precious metals increased nearly five-fold and the quantity of minted coin nearly quadrupled between 1492-1600.[19] Commodity prices also rose an estimated five times during the sixteenth century, according to Jacob. Another historian notes, "American gold caused such an

---

17. For annual production figures for gold since 1492, see Jastram, *The Golden Constant*, pp. 221-25. Also, see J. D. Magee, "The World's Production of Gold and Silver from 1493 to 1905," *Journal of Political Economy* (May 1909), pp. 50-58.

18. Jastram, *The Golden Constant*, p. 40.

19. William Jacob, *An Historical Inquiry into the Production and Consumption of the Precious Metals* (London: John Murray, 1831), vol. 2, pp. 41-114, particularly pp. 70, 87-88.

increase in gold supplies that the metal depreciated, sparking horrendous inflation felt not only in nonindustrial Spain but all over Europe."[20] But was inflation really that serious? A five-fold increase in precious metals and prices over a century amounts to an annual compounded rate of only 1.6 percent. Admittedly, some years had more inflation than others, but the overall trend throughout the sixteenth century seems far less inflationary than commonly believed.

The gold discoveries in California and Australia in the 1850s added substantially to the supply of gold. Miners extracted more metal in the next 20 years than they had during the previous 350 years! Yet, despite this prestigious outpouring, production never expanded the aggregate stock by more than 5 percent during the height of the gold rush in the 1850s.[21]

The opening of new mines in South Africa and other areas of the world in 1890-1910 resulted in annual growth rates of only between 3 and 4 percent. Since 1910, yearly increases in the stock of gold have increased typically at less than 2 percent.[22] Even with the tremendous rise in the price of gold since 1971, when the world went off the gold standard and fixed exchange rates, production has generally lagged behind GNP growth. Gold output actually declined throughout the inflationary 1970s. In the 1980s, the mining industry finally responded to lower production costs, new mining technology, and higher prices. Nevertheless, while gold output has increased an average 20 percent per annum since 1980 (see figure 2), mining companies have been hard pressed to increase the aggregate gold stock by more than 2 percent per annum.

Effects of Gold on World Monetary Stocks

A more liberal interpretation of monetary expansion under a pure gold standard can be obtained by comparing annual production figures with the world monetary stock of gold. The world

---

20. Jenifer Marx, *The Magic of Gold* (Garden City: New York: Doubleday, 1978), p. 325.

21. Jastram, *The Golden Constant*, pp. 221-225, and J. D. Magee, "The World's Production of Gold and Silver from 1493-1905," pp. 50-58.

22. Jastram, *The Golden Constant*, pp. 221-225, and Refus S. Tucker, "Gold and the General Price Level," *Review of Economic Statistics* (July 1934), p. 12.

Figure 2

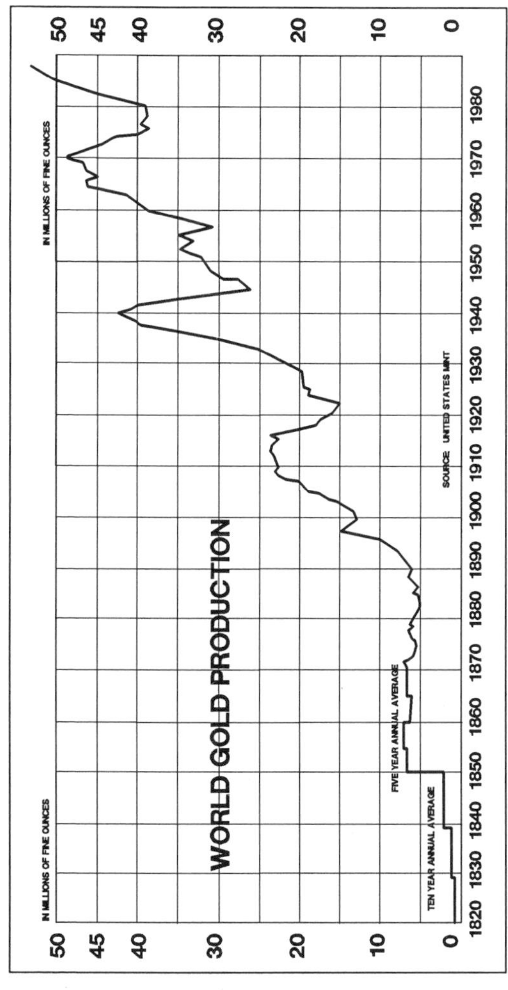
WORLD GOLD PRODUCTION
IN MILLIONS OF FINE OUNCES
IN MILLIONS OF FINE OUNCES
50
45
40
30
20
10
0
1820
1830
1840
1850
1860
1870
1880
1890
1900
1910
1920
1930
1940
1950
1960
1970
1980
TEN YEAR ANNUAL AVERAGE
FIVE YEAR ANNUAL AVERAGE
SOURCE UNITED STATES MINT

monetary stock is defined as the amount of gold held by governments and the public for the purpose of exchange and store of value, in either coin or bullion form. It does not include metal used in industry, art, and jewelry. According to a study by Refus Tucker covering the years 1800-1932, world monetary gold supplies increased between 1 and 12 percent (see "c" in figure 1). California-Australian discoveries increased the ratio to 12 percent in the early 1850s, and South African output increased the ratio to 7 percent around the turn of the century. However, under normal conditions, the ratio was typically below 5 percent. Since the opening of the South African mines, the percentage has gradually declined.[23] Historically, additions to monetary stocks have been substantially less than 5 percent because a large percentage of newly mined metal is used in industry and jewelry.

Impact of a Gold Rush on Domestic Money Supply

While there may be little monetary inflation worldwide under a pure gold standard, what about the impact of a gold supply shock domestically? For example, the California gold rush made the United States a major gold producer for the first time, with a pronounced effect on its money supply and prices. During 1849-54, the total hard currency increased at an annual rate of 13.9 percent.[24] This was when the United States was on the classic gold standard, at a time when all United States currency consisted of gold coins or paper money backed by gold bullion.

Thus, it is quite possible to experience a short-term inflationary impact under a gold rush. However, gold supply shocks have always been short-lived, lasting at most a decade. Moreover, it is important to note that new gold discoveries raise the monetary stock of a country to a new permanent level, from which they do not decline. Therefore, prices are likely to settle at a higher level than before the inflation began without creating a deflationary bust when the new gold rush is over.

---

23. Ibid.

24. U.S. Department of Commerce, *Historical Statistics of the United States, Colonial Times to 1970*, ser. 10 (Washington, D.C.: Government Printing Office, n. d.), pp. 420-423, 993.

In addition to the virtual elimination of monetary deflation and bank failure, some hard money advocates have pointed to the ability of such a system in combating business fluctuations.[25] Both Hayek and Rothbard have argued that though shifts in the production of specie may cause inflationary or deflationary effects on the overall price level, no business cycle necessarily develops as a result of a pure commodity standard.[26]

International Effects of the 100 Percent Standard

The stability of the domestic banking system also applies to stability in the international arena. Objections to the historical gold standard include its vulnerability to sudden deflations and specie drain threatening bank reserves domestically. Previously, we noted how a monetary deflation was virtually impossible under a pure gold standard. Yet economists frequently refer to the "specie-flow mechanism" to demonstrate that a domestic deflation is quite possible under gold. When a country inflates the money supply beyond specie, prices tend to rise, exports fall, imports rise, and the country suffers a gold drain. This trade imbalance and specie drain forces the country to reduce its money supply in an effort to restore stability.

Gold standard adherents argue that such a deflation is only possible if a country goes off the 100 percent gold standard and inflations the currency beyond its gold reserves. Professor Leland B. Yeager, in his dissertation topic on freely fluctuating exchange rates, discusses how a pure specie standard would maintain international order:

> Under a 100 per cent hard-money international gold standard, the currency of each country would consist exclusively of gold (or of gold plus fully-backed warehouse receipts for gold in the form of paper money and token coins). The government and its agencies would not have to worry about any drain on their reserves. The gold warehouses would never be embarrassed by requests to redeem paper money in gold, since each dollar of paper money in

25. Ibid., p. 284.

26. Friedrich Hayek, *Monetary Nationalism*, pp. 23-24, and Rothbard, *America's Great Depression* (Kansas City: Sheed and Ward, 1975), pp. 37-38. This will be discussed later at greater length.

> circulation would represent a dollar of gold actually in a warehouse. There would be no such thing as independent national monetary policies; the volume of money in each country would be determined by market forces. The world's gold supply would be distributed among the various countries according to the demands for cash balances of the individuals in the various countries. There would be no danger of gold deserting some countries and piling up excessively in others, for each individual would take care not to let his cash balance shrink or expand to a size which he considered inappropriate in view of his own income and wealth.
>
> Under a 100 per cent gold standard . . . the various countries would have a common monetary system, just as the various states of the United States now have a common monetary system. There would be no more reason to worry about disequilibrium in the balance of payments of any particular country than there is now reason to worry about disequilibrium in the balance of payments of New York City. If each individual (and institution) took care to avoid persistent disequilibrium in his personal balance of payments, that would be enough. . . . The actions of individuals in maintaining their cash balances at appropriate levels would 'automatically' take care of the adequacy of each country's money supply.[27]

In reference to the problems of deflation, contraction, and balance of payments crises, Yeager argues that:

> National fractional reserve systems are the real source of most of the difficulties blamed on the gold standard. . . . The difficulties arise because the mixed national currencies—currencies which are largely paper and only partly gold—are insufficiently international. The main defect of the historical gold standard is the necessity of 'protecting' national gold reserves. . . . In short, whether a Central Bank amplifies the effects of gold flows, or 'offsets' gold flows, its behavior is incompatible with the principles of the full-fledged gold standard. . . . Indeed, any kind of monetary management runs counter to the principles of the pure gold standard.[28]

---

27. Leland B. Yeager, "An Evaluation of Freely Fluctuating Exchange Rates," unpublished Ph.D. dissertation, Columbia University, 1952, pp. 9-10.

28. Ibid., pp. 11-17. For a critique of the gold exchange standard under the Bretton Woods agreement, see Joseph T. Salerno, "Gold and the International Monetary System: The Contribution of Michael A. Heilperin," in *The Gold Standard*, op. cit., pp. 81-111.

Objections to a Pure Specie Standard

Objections to a pure specie system of money come from a variety of directions. Opponents point to the many defects of specie and quarrel with many of the alleged benefits discussed above. Objections come from the "free banking" school, which argues that it is simply another unnecessary intervention by government into the affairs of private bankers; from the "Chicago School" and others (Friedman, Mints, Simons, and Fisher), who argue that it cannot achieve a perfectly stable price level and that it is far too expensive to operate; traditional neoclassical economists who argue that it would unduly restrain the functions of banking, cut profits to disparate levels and dry up sources of credit. In addition, they argue that it is too inflationary, insufficiently "elastic," and far too impractical to ever be tried.

These objections are often recognized by the 100 percent proponents, and their response is noted below.

The 100 Percent Rule and "Free Banking"

The "free banking" school, which encompasses in part the Banking School of England in the 1830-40s, as well as Adam Smith, William Brough, Ludwig von Mises, and Lawrence H. White, introduces a two-pronged attack on 100 percent banking. First, it is considered an infringement on personal liberty, and second, it does not allow the money supply to adjust to the "needs of business and trade."

The Question of Freedom and Fraud

Concerning this first point, it was the position of the free banking school that "it is among the elementary rights of an individual to make promises, and that each banker should be allowed to issue as many notes as he can get his customers to take, keeping such a reserve of metallic money, as he thinks, in his own private discretion, sufficient to enable him to redeem his promises."[29]

---

29. W. S. Jevons, *Money and Mechanism*, p. 308.

According to this reasoning, fractional reserve banking was not a fraudulent practice at all, as the 100 percent advocates contended. The proper level of reserves is simply a question of prudent banking practice. There should be nothing wrong with the issuance of banknotes beyond specie as long as they are convertible on demand into gold and silver—any other restriction on them being an infringement of "natural liberty."[30]

Mises sees no fraudulent behavior in the development of fractional reserve banking. He compares bank deposits with loaves of bread, stating: "A person who has a thousand loaves of bread at his immediate disposal will not dare to issue more than a thousand tickets each of which gives its holders the right to demand at any time the delivery of a loaf of bread. It is otherwise with money." But since money is never kept as a consumption item and is in fact passed from hand to hand without any attempt on the part of the public to redeem the money claim, the banker "is therefore in a position to undertake greater obligations than he would ever be able to fulfill."[31]

F. A. Walker does not dispute the ethics of fractional reserves—it's purely a "banking question"—and compares it to the risk of "collisions and boiler explosions involved in the use of steam cars and steamboats."[32] And Charles A. Conant compares banknotes to the commodity futures market in justifying uncovered notes: They are "simply an engagement to deliver metallic money . . . In this respect it does not differ from an engagement to deliver wheat, except that the article promised is of more general acceptability. . . . It is not necessary in either case that the signer of the engagement should possess the full amount of the commodity which he promises; it is only necessary that his reputation and other forms of property should inspire confidence in his ability to fulfill the promise."[33]

---

30. Adam Smith, *Wealth of Nations*, pp. 308, 313.

31. Ludwig von Mises, *Theory of Money and Credit*, p. 267.

32. F. A. Walker, *Money, In Its Relation to Trade and Industry* (New York: Henry Holt and Co., 1889), p. 270.

33. Charles A. Conant, *Money and Banking*, Vol. II, p. 20.

Walter E. Spahr, who supports a pre-1933 gold standard, often uses the analogy of a bridge to justify fractional reserve banking. "The builder of a bridge estimates approximately how many people will be using it daily. He builds the bridge on that basis and does not attempt to accommodate all the people in the city, should they all decide to cross the bridge simultaneously."[34] The banker, then, becomes an engineer-entrepreneur who tries to forecast what level of reserves is sufficient to meet current demands for redemption.

Free-banking advocate Lawrence H. White has written: "It is difficult to see why an analyst committed to the ethic of individual sovereignty, as Rothbard clearly is, would wish to prevent banks and their customers from making whatever sorts of contractual arrangements as are mutually agreeable." White references a typical old British banknote: "The Bank of XYZ 'promises to pay the bearer on demand one pound sterling.' There is no promise made about reserve-holding behavior. There is nothing to indicate that the note constitutes a warehouse receipt or establishes a bailment contract."[35] White states that the banknote actually constitutes a "conditional title," and the bank may, "consistent with title transfer, insert a clause into note and deposit contracts reserving to itself the option of delaying redemption."[36] Such practices are common among commercial banks and savings institutions today regarding passbook savings accounts.

In response to these arguments in favor of fractional reserve banking, 100 percent hard money advocates respond that these analogies are false and improper and that issuing notes beyond specie is a fraudulent practice. The fundamental basis for this argument is closely related to the legal relationship between the banker and the depositors. According to proponents, bankers are in reality custodians, not owners, of depositors' funds. Money deposited with a banker is still owned by the depositor, and can be

---

34. Spahr and Bill, eds., *A Proper Monetary and Banking System for the United States*, op. cit. Referred to in Rothbard, *The Case for 100 Percent*, p. 25.

35. Lawrence H. White, "Free Banking and the Gold Standard," *The Gold Standard*, op. cit., p. 120.

36. Ibid., p. 121.

withdrawn on demand by presenting the banknotes or by writing a check. Thus, the use of these deposited funds by the bankers, as was the practice of the goldsmiths, "was essentially unsound, if not actually dishonest and fraudulent. A warehouseman, taking goods deposited with him and devoting them to his own profit, either by use or by loan to another, is guilty of a tort, a conversion of goods for which he is liable in civil, if not criminal, law," according to Elgin Groseclose.[37]

Howard S. Katz notes in this regard: "When the original depositors brought their gold to the goldsmith, the moral-legal relationship was quite clear. The gold belonged to the depositor; the goldsmith-banker merely stored it and issued a paper receipt as proof of ownership. If the banker used the depositor's gold for some other purpose, he a was a thief. If he issued notes for which there was no gold, he was guilty of fraud."[38]

Katz makes a contrasting analogy of this moral-legal relationship in the case of men's hats and a hat check stand.

> Assume that all men's hats were the same, and in a given hotel there were continuous functions so that day in and day out there were always hats deposited with the hat check girl. (The hat check girl issued little tickets which served as receipts so that the men could claim their hats when they wanted them.) Suppose then, that the hat check girl noticed that it was very rare for a demand to come in for more than 50% of the hats at one time without this being offset by a new deposit of hats from new customers. Suppose further that an 'enterprising' hat check girl decided to sell 25% of the hats and pocket the money or—what amounts to the same thing—issue tickets for hats which don't exist and exchange those tickets for money. Such an event would clearly be fraudulent. The customers, who have a right to their hats, are being deceived. If the girl maintained that she was doing nothing wrong because the hats were her reserves and she maintained enough 'reserves' to meet the normal demand for hats, this argu-

---

37. Elgin Groseclose, *Money, The Human Conflict*, p. 178.

38. Howard S. Katz, *The Paper Aristocracy* (New York: Books in Focus, 1976), p. 65.

ment would not be valid. It is not valid with regard to bankers either.[39]

Katz is highly critical of the terms "reserves" and "convertibility." "The paper banknote," argues Katz, "was not a kind of money which was converted into gold. It was a receipt which was being *redeemed*. When you take your ticket to the hat check girl and demand your hat, you are not converting the ticket into a hat; similarly, when you take your claim check to the baggage department to claim your baggage, you are not converting your claim check into baggage. The ticket or claim check is simply a token of the department's promise that the hat or baggage in its possession is yours, and will give it back to you whenever you demand it."[40]

Rothbard disputes the comparison that Spahr makes between fractional reserve banking and the building of a bridge, where it is impossible for all the people to cross the bridge at the same time. He retorts:

> But the most critical fallacy of this analogy is that the inhabitants do not then have a legal claim to cross the bridge at any time. (This would be even more evident if the bridge were owned by a private firm.) On the other hand, the holders of money substitutes most emphatically do have a legal claim to their own property at any time they choose to redeem it. The claims must then be fraudulent, since the bank could not possibly meet them all. A bank that fails is therefore not simply an entrepreneur whose forecasts have gone awry. It is a business whose betrayal of trust has finally been publicly revealed.[41]

In principle, Rothbard compares the fractional reserve banker to an embezzler who

> takes money out of the company till to invest in some ventures of his own. Like the banker, he sees an opportunity to earn a profit on *someone else's assets*. The embezzler knows, let us say, that the

39. Ibid., pp. 65-66.
40. Ibid., p. 66.
41. Murray Rothbard, *The Case for 100 Percent*, p. 25.

> auditor will come on June 1 to inspect the accounts; and he fully intends to repay the "loan" before then. Let us assume that he does; is it really true that no one has been the loser and everyone has gained? I dispute this; a theft has occurred, and that theft should be prosecuted and not condoned. Let us note that the banking advocate assumes that something has gone wrong only if everyone should decide to redeem his property, only to find that it isn't there. But I maintain that the wrong—the theft—occurs at the time the embezzler takes the money, not at the later time when his "borrowing" happens to be discovered.[42]

In a footnote, Rothbard is careful not to accuse present-day bankers of conscious fraud or embezzlement; ". . . the institution of banking has become so hallowed and venerated that we can only say that it allows for legalized fraud, probably unknown to almost all bankers. As for the original goldsmiths that began the practice, I think our opinion should be rather more harsh."[43] Irving Fisher makes a similar caveat.[44]

Is "Free Banking" Destabilizing?

Apart from the question of fraudulent behavior of bankers, there has been considerable debate over whether "free banking," where banks are free to determine their own level of specie reserves, is stabilizing toward equilibrium or destabilizing over time. This question is frequently raised primarily because many 100 percent advocates view "free banking" as a second-best solution if 100 percent reserves are not imposed on the monetary system.

The Free Banking School argues that the redemption-on-demand clause combined with competition always insures that reserves will never fall to dangerous levels. Adam Smith, a strong supporter of "free banking," believes that there is a restraint to paper money expansion, limited by what is "necessary for transacting

42. Ibid., pp. 21-22. Note, however, that banking policy generally forbids the use of depositors' funds for personal bankers' use in an apparent effort to claim legitimacy in fractional reserve banking.

43. Ibid., p. 22n.

44. Irving Fisher, *100% Money*, pp. 18-19.

domestic business," and that if paper currency exceeds these "needs," the banks would be faced with runs and foreign demands for gold and silver. Thus, an equilibrium is established. Smith, however, never defines what he means by "paper which was over and above what could be employed in the circulation of the country."[45]

Sir Henry Parnell, member of the Banking School of thought, defends free banking ("wholly free from all legislative interference"), and uses the Scottish banking system as a prime example. According to Parnell, the Scottish banks regularly drew each other's checks through clearinghouses, and this frequent redemption system acted as an efficient check on the overissue of banknotes.

According to this system,

> Now if any bank A receives by such means more notes of bank B than B receives of A's notes, there will arise a clearing balance in favour of A, and A will require to be paid in gold out of B's reserves. So it is concluded that if one bank overissued its notes and the other banks would acquire positive balances against it, and the consequent drain on its reserves would pull it up in its expansion. This control by the way of the clearing mechanism was one which depended not on the public's presenting notes for redemption but on the banks' reciprocally doing so, and it was a check which was likely to work much more quickly than one which waited on the external drain of bullion set in motion by the falling foreign exchange rates.[46]

Parnell concludes: "It is this continual demand for coin, by the banks on one another, that gives the principle of convertibility full effect, and no such thing as an excess of paper or as a depreciation of its value can take place for want of a sufficiently early and active demand for gold."[47]

In the U.S., hard money advocate Condy Raguet argues that

---

45. Adam Smith, *Wealth of Nations*, pp. 284-87, 298.

46. Vera C. Smith, *Central Banking*, p. 63.

47. Sir Henry Parnell, "Observations on Paper Money, Banking and Overtrading . . . ," Pamphlet, 1827, p. 88.

frequent redemption of banknotes for specie would keep a check on note issue.[48]

Stanley Jevons, Robert Giffen, Charles Conant and others take the opposite point of view, and oppose free banking on the basis that it is self-destructive and that convertibility is not a sufficient deterrent to overissue of banknotes. Jevons states, "It would be of comparatively little use, however, for some banks to become more prudent and self-denying, while others are allowed to stretch their resources to the utmost possible point, and outbid the more prudent bank in the rates of dividends they pay."[49] Others agree. Mountifort Longfield argues that there is simply no check on the overissue of banknotes and that conservative banks are at the mercy of expanding, speculative banks.[50]

Charles A. Conant corroborates this point of view. "Where competition enters into the problem between banks otherwise upon equal footing, the bank which runs closest to the danger line in respect to the size of its metallic reserve without actually impairing public confidence, will make the largest profits." And so there is a strong tendency for banks to follow suit.[51]

Ludwig von Mises, perhaps the most vocal supporter of "free banking" in this century, maintains that privileged monopolistic banks, under state charters, are responsible in the main for overissue, bank runs, and economic disasters. Thus, "The establishment of free banking was never seriously considered precisely because it would have been too efficient in restricting credit expansion."[52]

According to Mises, there are two natural forces which limit the increase in fiduciary media: first, suspicions of the public which would increase redemptions and a possible run on the bank; and second, too rapid a rise in prices causing a move into "real values." Furthermore, under a multiplicity of independent

---

48. Condy Raguet, *Currency and Banking* (1839), passim.
49. W. S. Jevons, *Money and Mechanism*, p. 316.
50. Mountifort Longfield, "Banking and Currency," *Dublin University Magazine*, February 1840.
51. Charles A. Conant, *Money and Banking*, II, pp. 71-72.
52. Ludwig von Mises, *Human Action*, p. 441.

banks, if one bank overissues its fiduciary money, eventually the expansion must come to an end as their own clients seek to redeem their notes for real money to pay for goods and services. Moreover, "for such a multiplicity of independent coexisting banks the limits are narrower than those drawn for a single bank with an unlimited clientele."[53]

White argues that "a plurality of issuers minimizes the chances for large-scale errors in the money supply. . . . The overexpansive bank will discover that its specie reserves are drained away."[54]

Rothbard takes a similar stand, viewing "free banking" as a kind of second best solution to the problems of monetary systems. He writes,

> For a believer in free enterprise, a system of "free banking" undoubtedly has many attractions. Not only does it seem more consistent with the general institution of free enterprise, but Mises and others have shown that free banking would not lead to the infinite supply of money envisioned by such Utopian partisans of free banking as Proudhon, Spooner, Greene, and Meulen, but rather to a much "harder" and sounder money than exists when banks are controlled by a central bank. In practice, therefore, free banking would come much closer to the 100 percent ideal than the system we now have. And yet if "free trade in banking is free trade in swindling," then surely the soundest course would be to take the swindling out of banking altogether. Mises' sole argument against 100 percent banking is that this would admit the unfortunate precedent of government control of the banking system. But if fractional reserve banking is fraudulent, then it could be outlawed not as a form of administrative government intervention in the monetary system, but rather as a part of the general legal prohibition of force and fraud.[55]

Mises, Rothbard, and others all admit, however, that even with frequent redemption of banknotes by the public as well as

---

53. Ibid., pp. 436-37.

54. White, "Free Banking," *The Gold Standard*, pp. 121-22.

55. Murray Rothbard, *The Case for 100 Percent*, p. 26. See also, *What Has Government Done*, pp. 24-25, and *The Mystery of Banking*, pp. 111-24. Rothbard recently revised his position, especially with regard to the case of Scottish "free banking." See Rothbard, "The Myth of Free Banking in Scotland," *The Review of Austrian Economics* 2 (1987), pp. 229-45.

competing banks, a "perfect" 100 percent reserve could not be achieved. Mises himself confesses that free banking would "not hinder a slow credit expansion," but would only keep it from becoming a rapid credit expansion and it would avoid the after-effects of crises and depressions.[56]

Currency Elasticity and the Needs of Business

Many members of the "free banking" school of thought argue that a national currency should adjust to the "needs of trade." William Brough, for example, argues that a fractional reserve system, which fluctuates according to loan demand, is good for the economy because it provides an "elastic" currency which can easily expand or contract according to the needs of business. Both a purely metallic standard and a government paper-money standard lack this elasticity, according to Brough.[57] Adam Smith held similar notions.[58]

Later, such critics as F. A. Hayek and J. M. Keynes criticized the specie standard for its "inelasticity." In one case, interestingly enough, a strict inelastic supply of money is regarded as highly beneficial, in another case it is a major defect!

According to Keynes, the inelasticity of metallic money is a major flaw, especially under conditions of unemployment and the liquidity trap:

> It is interesting to notice that the characteristic which has been traditionally supposed to render gold especially suitable for use as a standard of value, namely, its inelasticity of supply, turns out to be precisely the characteristic which is at the bottom of the trouble.[59]

Keynes argues for the need of elasticity in the money supply:

> Thus, the characteristic that money cannot be readily produced by labour gives at once some prima facie presumption for the

56. Ludwig von Mises, *Human Action*, p. 443.
57. William Brough, *Open Mints*, pp. 73-74. Cf. Brace, *Gold Production*, p. 84.
58. Adam Smith, *Wealth of Nations*, pp. 284-85.
59. John Maynard Keynes, *The General Theory of Employment, Interest and Money* (New York: Harcourt, Brace & Co., 1936), pp. 235-36.

> view that its own rate of interest will be relatively reluctant to fall; whereas if money could be grown like a crop or manufactured like a motorcar, depressions would be avoided or mitigated because, if the price of other assets was tending to fall in terms of money, more labour would be diverted into the production of money.[60]

It is Keynes' contention that under the gold standard then in existence in the 1930s, where only a small portion of reserves was held in gold bullion, a fall in the price level would only stimulate production and employment "in a country of which gold-mining is the major industry." Under a 100 percent specie system, however, it might be distinctly different. Thus, Friedman makes the important premise that "under such a standard, an increased demand for money would be a demand for a commodity and hence an indirect demand for the factors of production used in producing it; hence, unemployment arising out of a liquidity trap of the Keynesian type would be impossible."[61] This assumes, of course, that there are no barriers in shifting employment and production to the specie-producing industries.

Hayek also rejects a pure gold standard in part because of its inability for production to respond quickly to "genuine" changes in demand for money.

> The great increases in the supply of gold in the past have in fact occurred when a prolonged scarcity has created a real need for them. The really serious objection against gold is rather the slowness with which its supply adjusts itself to genuine changes in demand. A temporary increase in the general demand for highly liquid assets, or the adoption of the gold standard by a new country, was bound to cause great changes in the value of gold while the supply adjusted itself only slowly. By a sort of delay action the increased supplies often became available only when they were no longer needed.[62]

---

60. Ibid., pp. 230-31.
61. Milton Friedman, *Monetary Stability,* p. 104n.
62. F. A. Hayek, *Individualism and the Economic Order,* p. 211.

Bullion supporters have offered several responses to this criticism. F. A. Walker, for example, disputes the idea that a fiduciary issue responds better to the needs of trade. On the contrary, Walker argues that a metallic currency is more "elastic." Thus,

> If an exceptional demand arises anywhere, gold or silver responds with an alacrity which would be unattainable by any article not possessing great value for its bulk, and not, at the same time, that article in which the values of all commodities are expressed for purposes of exchange. But while, in obedience to economical impulses, however slight, there may be more of such money in any one place, at one time than at another, the total amount is not, on that account, increased. . . . With a Convertible Paper Money, however, no such assurance exists. Enlarged local demand is not by a supply drawn from the general reservoir, to be returned again after the exigency is over to the common circulation, but by issues of local origin and local acceptance.[63]

In like manner, adjustments are made automatically when facing a seasonal change in the demand for money. Walker contends that "velocity would spontaneously rise in response to an increased demand for money, and he explained this point very responsibly."[64] On this subject, Mints notes:

> Rates of interest would rise as the seasonal peak in transactions was approached, and this fact might cause businessmen to economize on cash. However, a more important factor would be the build-up of cash balances by those who anticipated increased needs for cash later in the year, which is merely a way of saying that velocity would be relatively low at other times than those of the greatest need.[65]

Charles H. Carroll rejects the idea of elasticity entirely. He debunks the concept that "increasing trade necessarily requires an increase of money." Rather, Carroll sees the adjustments taking

---

63. F. A. Walker, *Money*, p. 417.
64. Lloyd W. Mints, *History of Banking Theory*, p. 236.
65. Ibid.

place in terms of changing prices. Increases in gold production would be compensated by rising prices, and vice versa, and "the universal supply of gold is not an important addition to wealth."[66]

The concept that the universal supply of specie money does not matter is promulgated by many hard money adherents, in addition to Carroll. Mises, for instance, maintains that an increase in the stock of money does not increase general welfare, but only changes the distribution of wealth through price changes: ". . . for it can only benefit a part of the community at the cost of a corresponding loss by the other part."[67] Rothbard also writes on this subject:

> An increase in the supply of money means merely that more units of money are doing the social work of exchange and therefore that the purchasing power of each unit will decline. Because of this adjustment, money, in contrast to all other useful commodities employed in production or consumption, does not confer a social benefit when its supply increases. The only reason that increased gold mining is useful, in fact, is that the large supply of gold will satisfy more of the nonmonetary uses of the gold commodity.[68]

Burdensome Restrictions on Banking

Several critics maintain that under the 100 percent proposal, banking would face such undue hardship that it would be practically legislated out of existence. Arthur Nussbaum, for example, states, "Only in a broad and non-technical sense may the relationship of the depository bank to the depositor be considered a fiduciary one. No trust proper or bailment is involved. The contrary view would lay an unbearable burden upon banking business."[69]

Mises makes a similar criticism on the cost of a 100 percent reserve system.

---

66. Charles H. Carroll, "The Gold of California and Paper Money," *Organization of Debt*, pp. 19-31.

67. Ludwig von Mises, *Theory of Money and Credit*, p. 208.

68. Murray Rothbard, *The Case of 100 Percent*, p. 28.

69. Arthur Nussbaum, *Money in the Law, National and International* (Brooklyn, N.Y.: Foundation Press, 1950), p. 105.

> Issuing money-certificates is an expensive venture. The banknotes must be printed, the token coins minted; a complicated accounting system for the deposits must be organized; the reserves must be kept in safety; then there is the risk of being cheated by counterfeit banknotes and checks. Against all these expenses stands only the slight chance that some of the banknotes issued may be destroyed and the still slighter chance that some depositors may forget their deposits. Issuing money-certificates is a ruinous business if not connected with issuing fiduciary media. In the early history of banking there were banks whose only operation consisted in issuing money-certificates. But these banks were indemnified by their clients for the costs incurred.[70]

Elsewhere, Mises uses even stronger language: "Prohibition of the issue of all notes except those with a full backing and of the lending of the deposits which serve as the basis of the cheque-and-clearing business would mean almost completely suppressing the note-issue and almost strangling the cheque-and-clearing system." Mises admits, however, that prohibition of fiat currency would not mean the "death sentence" for banking. Banks would continue to negotiate credit, borrowing for the purpose of lending.[71]

Jevons also writes concerning bank profit: "No banker could make a profit if he were obliged to put away the sovereigns deposited by a customer until that customer presented a cheque for them, nor would there usually be sufficient motive for desiring such a special pledge."[72]

Supporters of the 100 percent rule do not envision such a drastic curtailment of banking activity, however. Service charges would naturally be imposed, higher than what is now customary —although it is conceivable that these depository fees might be partially offset by other profitable activities of the banks in an effort to expand their market area. Rothbard responds to the overburdensome issue by stating:

70. Ludwig von Mises, *Human Action*, p. 435.
71. Ludwig von Mises, *Theory of Money and Credit*, pp. 323-25.
72. W. S. Jevons, *Money and Mechanism*, pp. 208-09.

> This argument points to the supposed enormous benefit ing; if these benefits were really so powerful, then surel sumers would be willing to pay a service charge for them, just as they pay for travelers' checks now. If they were not willing to pay the costs of the banking business as they pay the costs of all other industries useful to them, then that would demonstrate the advantages of banking to have been highly overrated.[73]

In another article, Rothbard elaborates:

> Almost all warehouses keep all the goods for their owners (100 percent reserve) as a matter of course—in fact, it would be considered fraud or theft to do otherwise. Their profits are earned from service charges to their customers. The banks can charge for their services the same way. If it is objected that customers will not pay the high service charges, then this means that the banks' services are not in very great demand, and the use of their services will fall to the levels that consumers find worthwhile.[74]

Price Stability and Gold Inflation

Many of the opponents to a pure specie standard have disputed the alleged claim that gold and silver production provides a relatively stable price level. We noted before how the supply of real money under this system is dependent entirely on the supply and demand for specie, and although the "demand is high, and the supply is low," there is no promise that the production of the precious metals will somehow coincide with a perfectly stable price level, either over the short term or the long term. The monetary gold stock may be steadily rising, but there is no guarantee that prices will be stable.

F. A. Walker refers to the price instability under gold over the long run. "We are not to expect," Walker says, "that the value of

---

73. Murray Rothbard, *Case for 100 Percent*, p. 27.

74. Murray Rothbard, *What Has Government Done*, pp. 21-22. Note also that, according to Adam Smith, the Bank of Amsterdam, a 100 percent bank of deposit, was highly profitable despite "exorbitant" fees. See Smith, *Wealth of Nations*, pp. 448-53. See also Dunbar, *Chapters on the Theory and History of Banking* (New York: Putnam, 1901), p. 104. Amsterdam's success, however, may have been primarily due to its monopolistic stature.

money will remain constant through any long period. One of the two parties to long contracts will, in all probably, lose while the other gains, by the change in values. The losses thus sustained may be slight; they may be serious, even ruinous."[75] Walker quotes Professor J. E. Cairnes on how serious these effects can be, referring to the period of history following gold discoveries in California and Australia:

> In almost every other aspect in which we contemplate the occurrence, it is fraught with inconvenience, hardship, and injustice, introducing uncertainty into mercantile dealings, disturbing contracts which were designed to be fixed, stimulating the spirit of commercial speculation, already too strong, and bringing unmerited loss upon classes who have the strongest claims on our sympathy and whom, upon social grounds, it is most desirable to sustain.[76]

However, the degree of instability created by the new gold discoveries may be grossly exaggerated by Cairnes and others due to the fractional reserve basis of the gold standard at the time, whose effects on the stock of money and prices were thereby exacerbated many times by the gold discoveries.

Harrison H. Brace questions the conclusions of Cairnes:

> Certainly it is that the alarmist predictions of Chevalier and his school were not realized. There were not those sudden rushes or jerks in price which, we are told, followed the great influx of precious metals from America in a former period. Business conditions were not the same in the nineteenth as in the sixteenth century. Business itself was of a much larger volume; communications were better; the world which could be affected by the new supplies was much larger.[77]

The speculative fever following the gold discoveries was exacerbated by "wildcat banking": "Abnormal speculation and abnormal credit go hand in hand. . . . But as time goes on it is found that

75. F. A. Walker, *Money*, p. 91.

76. John E. Cairnes, *Essays in Political Economy* (New York: Augustus M. Kelley, [1873] 1965). Quoted in Walker, *Money*, p. 149.

77. Harrison Brace, *Gold Production*, p. 23.

the demand was a false one—the loans in the banks which brought certain deposits into existence were not of a sound nature."[78]

In order to achieve price stability, Friedman points out that "In a stationary economy, production is needed solely to make good losses through wear and tear; in a growing economy, also to provide for an increase in the stock of money."[79] The stock of money, according to Friedman, "would have to grow about 4% a year to keep product prices roughly constant."[80]

J. M. Keynes expresses the views of many critics on the question of gold stability: "Material progress is more dependent now on the growth of scientific and technical knowledge, of which the application to gold-mining may be intermittent. Years may elapse without great improvement in the methods of extracting gold; and then the genius of a chemist may realise past dreams and forgotten hoaxes, transmuting base into precious like subtle, or extracting gold from sea-water as in the Bubble. Gold is liable to be either too dear or too cheap. In either case, it is too much to expect that a succession of accidents will keep the metal steady."[81]

In response to these challenges, the adherents of the 100 percent specie standard regard the national goal of price stability as an ephemeral goal which cannot be achieved in the real world under a market system, except by chance. Rather, their chief concern is whether specie is more stable than a fractional reserve system or even a 100 percent government fiat system. Price stability is a "utopian idea," according to Luigi Einaudi, "because it is impossible to formulate an unbiased price index which must form the

---

78. Ibid., pp. 81-82.

79. Milton Friedman, *Monetary Stability*, p. 5.

80. Ibid., pp. 104-05n.

81. J. M. Keynes, *Essays in Persuasion* (New York: Harcourt, Brace and Co., 1932), p. 201. Keynes is critical of two elements in monetary policies of the Western world: "the failure of the national currencies to remain stable in terms of what was supposed to be the standard of value, namely gold; and the failure of gold itself to remain stable in terms of purchasing power." *Idem.*, *A Tract on Monetary Reform* (London: Macmillan & Co., 1923), p. 140. When Keynes opposes a return to the "gold standard," he refers to the historical gold exchange standard, characterized by convertibility and a fixed rate in terms of gold. Considerable literature has been written on the defects of the historical gold standard, of which Keynes was a leader. But this is beyond the scope of this study.

basis of any price-stability goal." In addition, the stability of the general price level is "a naive and undemonstrable idea." Einaudi asks:

> Why should invariability of prices exist in a world where everything else continuously changes? Should we also aim at the invariability of each single price, which is manifestly absurd? Why intend the invariability of something as abstract as the general level of all prices? One should, however, recall that medieval man was inclined to look at the world in the light of eternity and immobility. The modern popular desire for a general price level that would be constant may be a fossil remnant of that medieval state of mind.[82]

Hard money supporters have generally recognized that their pure specie framework would mean periods of declining or rising prices in general, neither of which they regard as alarming.

History of Price Stability Under Gold

What about the historical evidence of price inflation under the gold standard? The record indicates that gold-induced price inflation was not that significant over the long term, even during periods when monetary standards involved fiduciary elements.

We noted earlier that prices rose steadily during the Spanish gold rush, increasing five fold during the sixteenth century. Debasement of European currencies may be partly responsible for this inflation, but even without allowing for currency depreciation, the average compounded rate of price inflation amounted to less than 2 percent per annum.

According to research by Roy Jastram, the British price level went through successive periods of inflation and deflation during its 300-year history under the gold standard. "Nevertheless," Jastram concludes, "gold maintains its purchasing power over long periods of time, for example, half-century intervals.[83] This conclusion led him to title his book, *The Golden Constant*.

According to research by Michael David Bordo, the wholesale price index was relatively more stable under the classic gold stan-

---

82. Luigi Einaudi, "Theory of Imaginary Money," in Lane and Riemersma, *Enterprise*, pp. 152-53.

83. Jastram, *The Golden Constant*, p. 132.

dard in Great Britain (1821-1914) and the United States (1834-1861 and 1879-1933) than afterwards when both countries adopted a far greater discretionary fiat money standard, see figures 3a and 3b. In both countries, the trendline was slightly deflationary under the classic gold standard.[84]

Friedman and Schwartz also conclude: "The blind, undesigned, and quasi-automatic working of the gold standard turned out to produce a greater measure of predictability and regularity—perhaps because its discipline was impersonal and inescapable—than did deliberate and conscious control exercised within institutional arrangements intended to promote stability."[85]

Critics of gold may grant the argument that price changes appeared to be relatively more moderate under the classic gold standard, but they argue, on the other hand, that "comparisons of per capita income growth and unemployment indicate that the gold standard had no obvious superiority over recent monetary arrangements; if anything the opposite is true."[86]

The High Cost of Production: Specie as a Waste of Resources?

One of the most popular arguments against the gold standard, as well as any commodity standard, is that the cost of producing gold or another commodity for monetary purposes is very expensive. This argument, probably more than any other, has been the basis for declining support for specie as a monetary numeraire, at least from an economic point of view.

The idea of a commodity standard as an expensive "waste of resources" is a remarkably old idea and was a view held by Adam Smith and David Ricardo. Adam Smith suggests that the replacement of gold and silver with paper notes would result in a less expensive money supply, and would serve equally well. He compares the precious metals to a road where all the corn has to come to mar-

---

84. Michael David Bordo, "The Gold Standard: Myths and Realities," in Barry N. Siegel, ed., *Money in Crisis*, pp. 211-14.

85. Milton Friedman and Anna J. Schwartz, *A Monetary History of the United States, 1867-1960* (Princeton: Princeton University Press, 1963), p. 10.

86. Barry Eichengreen, "Editor's Introduction," in Eichengreen, editor, *The Gold Standard in Theory and History* (New York: Methuen, 1985), p. 8, *passim*.

Figure 3a

Figure 3a
Wholesale Price Index
United Kingdom, 1880 - 1979

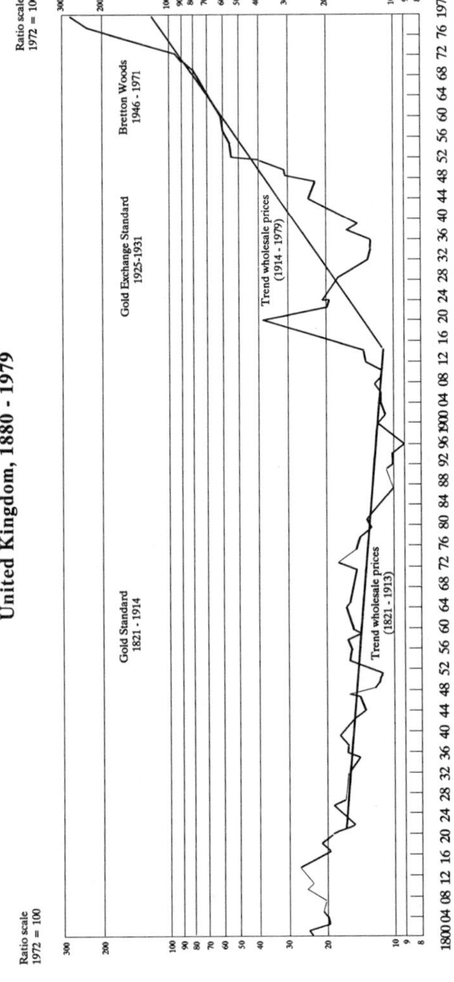

Note: Prepared by Federal Reserve Bank of St. Louis

Source: Michael David Bordo, "The Gold Standard: Myths and Realities," in **Money in Crisis**, Barry N. Siegel, ed. (Pacific Institute for Public Policy Research, 1984), p. 212.

Figure 3b

Figure 3b
Wholesale Price Index
United States, 1880 - 1979

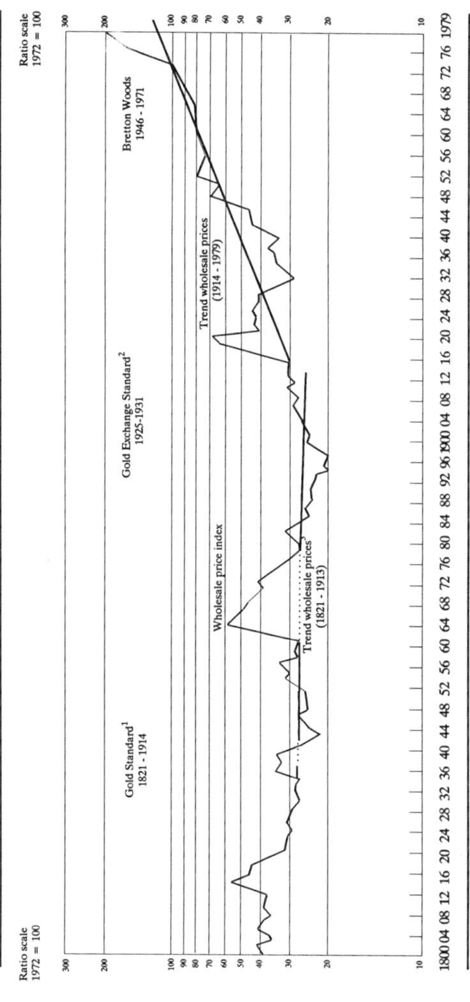

1. Wxcludes 1838-1843 when specie payments were suspended.

2. United States imposes gold export embargo from September 1917 to June 1919.

3. Broken line indicates years excluded in computing trend.

Note: Prepared by Federal Reserve Bank of St. Louis

Source: Michael David Bordo, "The Gold Standard: Myths and Realties," in **Money in Crisis**, Barry N. Siegel, ed. (Pacific Institute for Public Policy Research, 1984), p. 213.

ket, but on which nothing grows.[87] Ricardo held similar views. His ideal monetary system excludes the use of metallic money entirely from domestic use, replaced by paper money at a minimal cost.[88]

After referring to the views of Smith and Ricardo, Mises continues this classical position. The use of fiduciary money, argues Mises, has kept Western countries from diverting valuable labor and capital to mining production, which would have meant suffering for the "welfare of the community." The expense of the production of specie is one of the chief reasons why Mises rejects the full metallic standard.[89]

In *Human Action*, Mises reaffirms this viewpoint, based on the conclusion that money is singularly different from all other economic goods in that the quantity of money does not matter and is "always sufficient to secure for everybody all that money does and can do." Consequently, "From the point of view of this insight, one may call wasteful all expenditures incurred for increasing the quantity of money. The fact that things which could render some other useful services are employed as money and thus withheld from these other employments appears as a superfluous curtailment of limited opportunities for want-satisfaction." Mises does, however, make an important reservation, though entirely on political grounds: "If one looks at the catastrophic consequences of the great paper money inflations, one must admit that the expensiveness of gold production is the minor evil."[90] Such a political observation is not sufficient to persuade Mises to favor a pure gold standard, but it does reflect his support for "free banking."[91]

F. A. Hayek, Mises' counterpart, views the high cost of gold production as a "serious objection" to the gold standard. He states: "In a securely established world State with a government immune against the temptations of inflation it might be absurd to spend enormous effort in extracting gold out of the earth if cheap tokens would render the same service as gold with equal or great efficiency."[92]

87. Adam Smith, *Wealth of Nations*, Book II, pp. 28, 78.

88. David Ricardo, "Proposals for an Economical and Secure Currency," *Works*, p. 397ff.

89. Ludwig von Mises, *Theory of Money and Credit*, pp. 298-99, 323.

90. Ludwig von Mises, *Human Action*, pp. 421-22.

91. Ibid.

92. F. A. Hayek, *Monetary Nationalism and International Stability*, pp. 74-75. Cf. Wicksell, *Lectures on Political Economy*, p. 123.

Henry C. Simons refers to the miners under a gold standard as "sellers of redundant, useless hoards," resulting in the "squandering of world resources in gold production."[93] And Paul Samuelson reflects modern sentiment in saying, "How absurd to waste resources digging gold out of the bowels of the earth, only to inter it back again in the vaults of Fort Knox, Kentucky!"[94]

Milton Friedman provides a lucid explanation of this point of view. "The fundamental defect of a commodity standard," according to Friedman, "from the point of view of the society as a whole, is that it requires the use of real resources to add to the stock of money." This fact is a strong incentive to introduce fiduciary elements into the monetary system.[95] The economic cost to mine metallic money is, on the whole, "by no means negligible." Gold production would be very expensive even if a stable price level were to be achieved, argues Friedman. The "stock of money would have to grow by about 4% a year to keep product prices roughly constant," and "The use of so large a volume of resources for this purpose establishes a strong social incentive in a growing economy to find cheaper ways to provide a medium of exchange." On the other hand, a fiduciary currency "would involve a negligible use of real resources to produce the medium of exchange. . . ."[96]

Pesek and Saving, in their monetary textbook, *The Foundations of Money and Banking*, offer a graphic explanation of the issues involved through the use of the economic tools of supply and demand.[97]

First of all, Pesek and Saving examine the economics of a commodity money such as gold. They compare competitive conditions with the monopolistic conditions of gold production. Figure 4 is reproduced from the text.

The graph shows a specific stock of gold money in some specified year. The equilibrium stock of money is assumed to be q_e and the price is p_e, which represents the array of goods and services

93. Henry C. Simons, *Economic Policy*, p. 262.

94. Paul Samuelson, *Economics* (New York: McGraw-Hill, 1970, 8th ed.), p. 700.

95. Milton Friedman, "Should There be an Independent Monetary Authority?", *Monetary Stability*, p. 221.

96. Milton Friedman, *Monetary Stability*, pp. 5-7.

97. Boris P. Pesek and Thomas R. Saving, *The Foundations of Money and Banking* (New York: MacMillan, 1968), p. 60.

Figure 4

Comparison of Competitive and Monopolistic Money Production

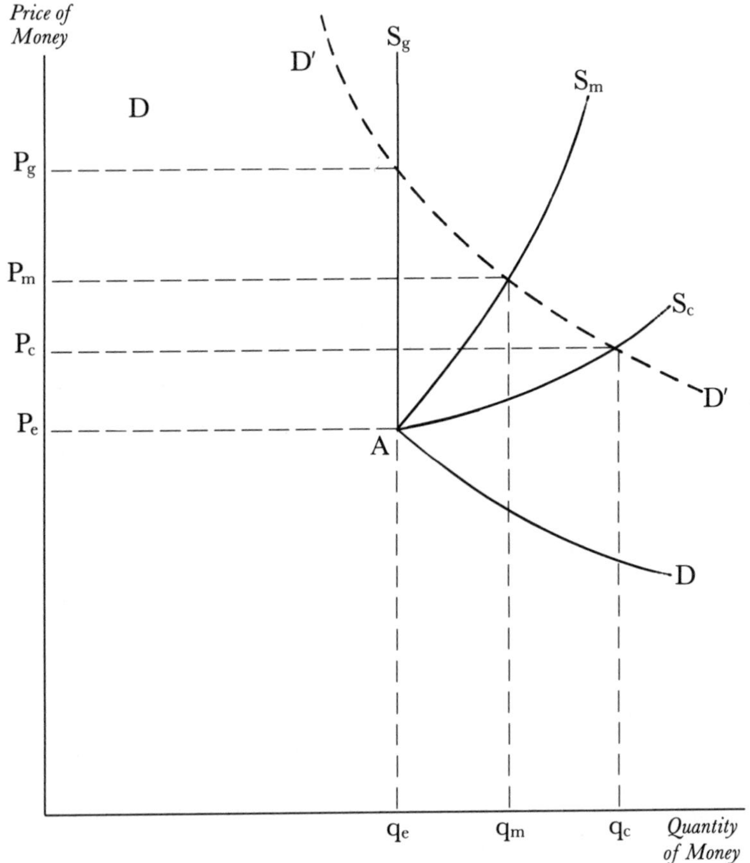

Source: Boris P. Pesek and Thomas R. Saving, *The Foundations of Money and Banking* (New York: MacMillan, 1968), p. 60.

that money will buy. Now, suppose that the demand for money increases from DD to D′D′. Assume that the competitive supply schedule is S_cS_c, where the subscript "c" denotes the competitive supply function. As the graph shows, an increase in the demand for money will increase the output of commodity money from q_e to q_c. If the money industry is monopolized, however, the supply function will be steeper (S_mS_m). The same shift of the demand function will cause the stock of money to increase by less than the competitive industry—to only q_m. Also, as the graph shows, with a smaller stock of money, the price of money will be higher p_m (i.e., prices of goods and services drop).

Unlike normal commodities, where monopolization is beneficial to the monopolist and harmful to the rest of society, a commodity money has a peculiar characteristic that makes its monopolization "desirable" from an economic point of view, according to Pesek and Saving. This unique quality is that "money goods . . . have a flow of services that is directly proportional to their price. This means that we can increase the ability of the money stock to provide (us) the services of a medium of exchange by enlarging the stock *or* by increasing its price." This is essentially the point that Mises demonstrates, i.e., that money is neither a consumption good nor a production good because the loss of money does not constitute a loss in general welfare, and "the economic position of mankind remains the same" (speaking only of the monetary, and not the industrial or artistic, use of the commodity-money).[98]

Thus, Pesek and Saving conclude,

> Monopolization, by reducing the output of the money commodity, releases the resources that would be used to produce the money commodity for other uses, *without* affecting the real income yielded by the money. Because monopolization of the output of money does not diminish the volume of services yielded by money and does, by restricting output and thus releasing resources for other uses, increase the volume of services yielded by other goods, it is easy to show that monopolization of the money

98. Ludwig von Mises, *Theory of Money and Credit*, p. 85.

> industry is desirable. (Note that if we object to the monopoly profits of the money producer, we can always tax them away, or even more simply, entrust the monopoly to the government itself.)

Pesek and Saving elaborate, using the graph:

> A competitive money industry that increases the output of the money commodity as a result of an increase in demand . . . is wasting resources (raw materials, man-hours, machine-hours). . . . Monopoly, by restricting the increase in stock (equilibrium stock is raised only to q_m), takes a step in the right direction. However, if an increase to q_c is wasteful, surely an increase to q_m is also wasteful, only less so. And, indeed, this is the case. If the government simply outlawed any additional production of money and thus gave us the supply function S_gS_g . . . , the desired increase in the services of money could be brought about entirely by changes in the price of money and no resources need be used.[99]

It is only one step further to realize, Pesek and Saving reason, that "if the quantity of units of money in existence doesn't matter," then "the material money is made of doesn't matter either." And the economic case can then be made for fiat money, under the monopoly power of the government. Even so, warn Pesek and Saving, "Unfortunately, the negligible production cost of modern money has its disadvantages. It has allowed governments to abuse their monopoly power in money production."[100] This in no way detracts from the *economic* arguments favoring fiat currency, however.

Until recently, the proponents of the pure gold standard have said little in opposition to this particular argument against a commodity-money, which as we have noted, is perhaps the most damaging economic argument against specie. Francis A. Walker is one of the few economists to comment in support of gold and to dismiss this alleged flaw in the gold standard. Replying to those who see "waste" in monetary gold, Walker replies:

---

99. Pesek and Saving, *Foundations*, pp. 61-62.
100. Ibid., p. 9.

> Is the bridge which bears up the train of freight or passengers less busy than the snorting, puffing engine which draws the cars? Are blocks of stone unused when laid deep under the ground in the foundation of a building which serves the purposes of industry, of art, or of government? Surely there is lack of scientific imagination in that view of the gold in the vaults of the Bank which regards it as idle and unused, when its true and faithful symbols are running their busy course above ground and outside the walls, effecting the daily exchanges of thirty millions of people.[101]

Recently, however, free-market economist Roger W. Garrison challenged the resource cost thesis of the gold critics. Garrison argues that with or without a gold standard, the resource costs of gold production are "unavoidable." He writes:

> The imposition of a paper standard does not cause gold to lose its monetary value. . . . Gold continues to be mined, refined, cast or minted, stored, and guarded; the resource costs continue to be incurred. In fact, a paper standard administered by an irresponsible monetary authority may drive the monetary value of gold so high that more resource costs are incurred under the paper standard than would have incurred under a gold standard. Market processes operating since antiquity have identified gold as the premier monetary commodity, and until the market's adoption of an alternative standard causes the value of gold to fall to a level that reflects only the nonmonetary uses of gold, these resource costs cannot be avoided."[102]

The Economics of an "Ideal" Standard: A Full Specie Standard Versus a Full Fiat Standard

Close similarities have been drawn throughout this work between the 100 percent specie or commodity standard and the 100 percent fiat standard as proposed by Irving Fisher and perpetuated by the Chicago School of Simons, Friedman, et al. Both pro-

---

101. F. A. Walker, *Money*, p. 528.

102. Roger W. Garrison, "The Costs of a Gold Standard," *The Gold Standard*, op. cit., p. 70. Friedman and Schwartz have recently acknowledged this point. See Friedman and Schwartz, "Has Government Any Role in Money?" in Anna J. Schwartz, *Money in Historical Perspective* (Chicago: University of Chicago Press, 1987), p. 310.

grams would strictly separate the functions of money creation and lending activities. Both would prohibit fractional reserves on demand deposits, reducing the deposit role of banks to literal warehouses of money, where 100 percent reserves would be required. Banks would have to rely on their own capital and accumulated surplus, if they desired to participate in credit transactions (or they could operate as financial intermediaries). No credit creation could take place from demand deposits, however (this would include nominal time deposits that permitted withdrawals on demand). Both specie and fiat standards would eliminate the need for federal deposit insurance.

The two standards differ essentially in two respects. First, they differ in emphasis and fundamental philosophy. The Chicago School views the 100 percent money proposal as a "technique"—an efficient, useful tool of the government in controlling the money supply and eliminating the "inherent instability" of fractional reserve banking, unhindered by lags or friction in the banking system. On the other hand, the hard money school sees the present fractional reserve system as not only inherently unstable, but a highly fraudulent and immoral practice of banking deception on the public. The return to 100 percent specie is regarded as a return to the free market in money and the full restoration of property rights for depositors.

The second important difference is, of course, the fact that one standard favors a commodity chosen over the years by the market as the medium of exchange (i.e., gold and silver), and the other chooses a paper standard, unbacked by any commodity, completely managed by the government's central bank. In the first case, the government is severely limited in manipulating the stock of money; in the second case, the government is central to the whole monetary framework and is in complete control of the monetary medium, and without it, the fiat standard would quickly disintegrate as all individuals sought to print their own paper currency.

There are numerous and complex reasons why a full, uninhibited specie standard has lost its standing among the monetary systems of the modern world, allowing a gradual shift in favor of a fiduciary medium of exchange. But aside from any political considerations to explain this fact, the overriding *economic* reason for abandoning specie in favor of unbacked paper has been the cost-justification factor. The production of gold and silver as monetary metals has been regarded as too heavy a financial burden on society, especially in contrast to the negligible cost of paper substitutes. This is the nub of the economic argument.

Murray Rothbard and Roger Garrison, among others, have made an attempt to override this principal issue by seeking to demonstrate the costly defects of a government fiat standard, whether in the form of a fractional reserve system or a 100 percent fiat reserve system, compared to a pure gold standard.

The economic argument against a full or partial fiat monetary standard revolves around the Austrian theory of business cycles as developed by Mises and Hayek and recently reinterpreted by Rothbard and other free-market economists. According to the Austrian economists, a fiat paper standard causes a grave misallocation of resources far worse than the alleged costs of a specie standard.

According to Hayek, who is the foremost theorist of this so-called "monetary malinvestment theory," there is a balance between producer goods and consumer goods. Equilibrium is established when there is little or no tendency toward the lengthening or shortening of the structure of production. This structure of production is seen as a series of "stages" starting with raw commodities and producers' or "higher order" capital goods and ending with final consumer goods.[103] Aggregate equilibrium is reached where there exists equilibrium between the supply and demand for both consumer goods and producer goods.

This equilibrium is disturbed whenever there are changes in the money supply or the public's saving/investment patterns. For example, if increased savings takes place *before* investment, then a

---

103. See. F. A. Hayek, *Prices and Production* (London: Routledge and Kegan Paul, 1935). Also, Mises, *Theory of Money and Credit*, and Eugen von Böhm-Bawerk, *Positive Theory of Capital* (South Holland, Ill.: Libertarian Press, 1959).

shift occurs in resources going from the production of consumption goods to investment goods. Consumption falls while investment rises, and there is little change in the price level.

On the other hand, if investment comes *before* savings through artificial credit expansion, there will be an expansion of investment *without* a change in consumption-savings patterns. As the structure of production becomes more roundabout, a boom begins and prices and costs tend to rise.

The business cycle is created, according to this thesis, by an expansion of the money supply through bank credit—either through the purchase of government securities by the Federal Reserve Open Market Committee or through lower reserve requirements and additional lending by the banking community. This effect can be accomplished by the 100 percent fiat reserve standard as well as by a fractional reserve banking system.

The increase in the money supply is first felt on the loan market in terms of increased supply of investment funds. The immediate effect is to reduce interest rates below what they would have attained otherwise. This creates a rise in investment expenditures relative to consumption expenditures—or, in other words, a drop in the uniform rate of discount will increase the demand-price schedule for durable capital goods relative to the demand-price schedule for present consumption goods. In purely Austrian terms, the capital structure is lengthened when businessmen use their newly acquired funds and invest them in the "higher order" production goods. As a result, this new demand schedule bids up the prices of capital goods—particularly the more durable goods—and causes a shift in investment from the "lower" (near the consumer) to the "higher" orders of production (farthest from the consumer).

This is essentially the "boom" pattern of the business cycle. But, as noted above, the expansion takes place most heavily in the durable goods industries and in the factors of production required to handle this increase demand (particularly raw materials). The boom eventually permeates the economy, but the markets closest to the consumer are least affected in this initial period of expansion.

The expansion period of the cycle does not last, however. In fact, according to this Austrian theory, the monetary expansion is "self-reversing" on the economy. Eventually, the increase in bank money sifts downward to the factors of production in the form of wages, rents, and interest. As this new money-income is spent, consumption demand begins to increase. Why? Because, according to the Austrians, the additional income is spent based on the individuals' *old* consumtion/savings patterns. Because the increase in investment funds was created by government fiat rather than out of the increased savings of the public, the assumption is made that the time preference and savings habits of the factors of production have not changed. Therefore, these factor-owners bid up the price of consumption goods ("lower orders") relative to capital goods ("higher orders").

The increase in the demand for consumer goods is met with no previous expansion in the supply of consumer goods, and thus consumer goods prices rise. This results in what is often called "forced savings" on the part of the consuming public.[104]

Finally, the consumer goods industries see profits rising and increase their output. Meanwhile, the demand for investment goods falls and the capital goods industries see their profits drop and interest rates climb as businesses scramble for liquidity. The upper turning point in the business cycle has been reached. The expected increased demand for the higher capital goods, which served as the basis for increased investments by entrepreneurs, proves to be lacking.

This portion then initiates the "contraction" or "bust" period of the business cycle. In Rothbard's words, "Capital goods industries will find that their investments have been in error: that what they thought profitable really fails for lack of demand by their entrepreneurial customers. Higher orders of production have turned out to be wasteful, and the malinvestment must be liquidated."[105] The boom, then, turns out to be a false prosperity which cannot continue forever.

---

104. Maurice W. Lee, *Macroeconomics: Fluctuations, Growth, and Stability* (Homewood, Ill.: Richard D. Irwin, 1971), p. 225.

105. Murray Rothbard, *America's Great Depression*, p. 18.

Gerald P. O'Driscoll, Jr., and Sudha R. Shenoy summarize this Austrian critique of the effects of fiat credit expansion:

> Monetary expansion began by lowering interest rates. Entrepreneurs, misled by the uncoordinated price signals, attempted to reduce all marginal rates of return to the same level. But in attempting to do so, they actually drove up ex post returns on some goods to levels higher than these interest rates. Monetary expansion thus induces disproportionalities in the production of capital goods that are revealed in the depression: there is overproduction in some lines, underproduction in others. . . .
>
> Monetary expansion thus sets in train an unsustainable change in the pattern of production, a change that must eventually be modified and reversed. Initially, as money incomes rise, the effects of the expansion may appear to be beneficial. But it is now that the unsustainable misallocations are being made, as prices of unfinished products rise relative to consumer goods prices. As the money permeates through the system, this relative price change is reversed, and consumer goods prices rise. The cluster of misallocations now stands revealed in the form of losses and unemployment, additional to those necessary for the continuous adaptation of production to changing circumstances. More specifically, resources become unemployed in stages furthest from consumption. This unemployment is reduced as consumer goods production picks up. Continuous monetary expansion can only perpetuate this cyclical discoordination in the capital structure and thus raise losses and unemployment above the level they would otherwise reach.[106]

Prior to this presentation of the Austrian view of the business cycle, hard money proponents usually explained the boom-bust cycle which frequently accompanied fractional reserve and "wildcat" banking by means of a specie-flow mechanism. Charles H.

106. Gerald P. O'Driscoll, Jr. and Sudha R. Shenoy, "Inflation, Recession, and Stagflation," in Edwin G. Dolan, ed., *The Foundations of Modern Austrian Economics* (Kansas City: Sheed & Ward, 1976), pp. 199-200. O'Driscoll and Shenoy offer interesting contrasts between Austrian interpretations of inflationary recession and Keynesian and Monetarist points of view.

Carroll, Daniel Raymond, David Hume and others "declared that the banks first expanded the currency, thus causing rising prices and speculation, and that this fact caused an outflow of specie in the wake of which came contraction, business losses, and failures."[107]

However, F. A. Walker, in his chapters on the effects of changes in the money supply, adopts a quasi-Austrian view of the business cycle. He notes, for example, that as to the cause of depression, "It is not, however, general over-production, but only over-production in certain lines. . . ."[108] Overexpansion does not take place in consumption goods, argues Walker: "The staple industries, and especially those producing the absolute necessaries of life, will never be suspended."[109]

German Economist Philip Joseph Geyer is one of the few hard money advocates to promulgate an Austrian picture of the business cycle as related to bank credit. Uncovered banknotes are, according to Geyer, "artificial" capital (*kunstliches Kapital*). Real capital, called "natural" (*naturliches*), is based entirely on completely covered note issues based on 100 percent specie reserves. Uncovered notes or "artificial" capital create a crisis from the phenomenon of overproduction.[110]

Criticisms of the Austrian Theory of the Business Cycle

Numerous criticisms have been made against the Hayek-Mises theory of the business cycle. One of the alleged defects is that the cycle theory assumes "full employment" of resources and factors of production. Maurice Lee argues that the full employment assumption is critical at the upper turning point of the cycle, and that without it, the theory is dubious.[111] On this point, Rothbard responds by arguing that "credit expansion generates the

---

107. Lloyd W. Mints, *History of Banking Theory*, p. 157.
108. Francis A. Walker, *Money, Trade and Industry*, p. 121.
109. Ibid., pp. 131-32.
110. Vera C. Smith, *Central Banking*, p. 108.
111. Maurice W. Lee, *Macroeconomics*, pp. 226-27.

business cycle regardless of the existence of unemployed factors."[112] While he states that additional credit expansion will simply create more distortions and malinvestments, further explanation would be helpful.

Gottfried Haberler and many others have referred to this Hayek-Mises theory as a "monetary overinvestment theory."[113] According to Mises, this is inaccurate: "The essence of the credit-expansion boom is not overinvestment, but investment in wrong lines, i.e., malinvestment on a scale for which the capital goods available do not suffice."[114]

Alvin Hansen, in his well-known work, *Business Cycles and National Income*, is critical of what has become known as the "Ricardo Effect" in the Hayekian cycle framework. The Ricardo Effect occurs as the boom advances to its later stages. At this point, Hayek predicts a decline in real wage rates as consumer prices start to climb. As this period proceeds, it becomes increasing profitable to substitute labor for machinery (the Ricardo Effect). This action reduces the roundabout process of production and introduces the downward cycle. Hansen disputes the argument that real wage rates fall during the later portion of the boom, and offers some statistical studies which show the contrary.[115]

Business Cycle Under Pure Gold Standard

In sharp contrast to the 100 percent fiat standard, it is Rothbard's contention that a 100 percent specie standard does not elicit the same cyclical patterns that characterize a fiat standard.

According to Rothbard, a boom-bust cycle cannot be generated by an increase in gold money under a pure gold standard. Monetary changes are not "self-reversing." In arguing this position, which is in sharp contrast with traditional views of many hard money supporters such as Mises, he states:

---

112. Murray Rothbard, *Great Depression*, p. 34.

113. Gottfried Haberler, *Prosperity and Depression* (Geneva: League of Nations, 1939, 2nd ed.), Chapter 3.

114. Ludwig von Mises, *Human Action*, p. 556.

115. Alvin Hansen, *Business Cycles and National Income* (New York: W. W. Norton & Co., 1964), pp. 392-93.

> One crucial distinction between a credit expansion and entry of new gold onto the loan market is that bank credit expansion distorts the market's reflection of the pattern of voluntary time preferences; the gold inflow embodies changes in the structure of voluntary time preferences. Setting aside any permanent shifts in income distribution caused by gold changes, time preferences may temporarily fall during the transition period before the effect of increased gold on the price system is completed. On the other hand, time preferences may temporarily rise. The fall will cause a temporary increase in saved funds, an increase that will disappear once the effects of the new money on prices are completed.
>
> Here is an instance in which savings may be expected to increase first and then decline. There may certainly be other cases in which time preferences will change suddenly on the free market, first falling, then increasing. The latter change will undoubtedly cause a "crisis" and temporary readjustment to malinvestments, but these would be better termed irregular fluctuations than regular processes of the business cycle. Furthermore, entrepreneurs are trained to estimate changes and avoid error. They can handle irregular fluctuations, and certainly they should be able to cope with the results of an inflow of gold, results which are roughly predictable. They could not forecast the results of a credit expansion, because the credit expansion tampered with all their moorings, distorted interest rates and calculations of capital. No such tampering takes place when gold flows into the economy, and the normal forecasting ability of entrepreneurs is allowed full sway. We must, therefore, conclude that we cannot apply the "business cycle" label to any processes of the free market. Irregular fluctuations, in response to changing consumer tastes, resources, etc., will certainly occur, and sometimes there will be aggregate losses as a result. But the regular, systematic distortion that invariably ends in a cluster of business errors and depression—characteristic phenomena of the "business cycle"—can only flow from intervention of the banking system in the market.[116]

F. A. Hayek takes a remarkably similar stand on this issue. In his *Monetary Nationalism and International Stability*, Hayek develops

116. Murray Rothbard, *Great Depression*, p. 38.

the international economics of a "purely metallic currency."[117] His model includes two countries, A and B, both of which use metallic coins which "are freely and without cost interchangeable at the mints." In this model, he predicts the effects on prices and production when someone who used to spend money on products in Country A now decides to spend money on products in Country B. The result is that there will be an "adverse balance of trade for A." In A, somebody's money receipts decrease, and in B, another's increases. As a result, country A's imports from B fall, or A's exports rise. The flow of money goes from A to B. "It will be prices and incomes of particular individuals and particular industries which will be affected and the effects will not be essentially different from those which will follow any shifts of demand between different industries or localities."[118]

Hayek then suggests that this pure metallic standard will be either deflationary or inflationary overall, but there should be no business cycle: "In particular there is no reason why the changes in the quantity of money within an area should bring about those merely temporary changes in relative prices which, in the case of a real inflation, lead to misdirections of production—misdirections because eventually the inherent mechanism of these inflations tend to reverse these changes of relative prices." Hayek also suggests that under a "homogeneous international currency," an outflow of money from A and an inflow into B will not necessarily cause a rise in the interest rates in A and a fall in B, but he does not elaborate.[119]

Summary

The 100 percent specie standard provides numerous advantages, according to partisans, over present monetary and banking arrangements. These advantages include: a system consistent with market values of individuals and full property rights of bank customers, independence from government interference into mone-

117. F. A. Hayek, *Monetary Nationalism*, pp. 4-25.
118. Ibid., p. 23.
119. Ibid., pp. 24-25.

tary affairs, avoidance of monetary inflation and currency debasement, harmony and order in international financial affairs, trade and specie flow, economic and banking stability domestically, virtual elimination of bank runs, unsound speculative banking schemes, and the business cycle.

Despite these highly idealistic claims, the 100 percent specie idea has drawn persistent criticism over the years. Indeed, opponents have not only offered severe criticism of the 100 percent plan, but have quarreled over the alleged advantages as well. The "free banking" school—from Adam Smith to Ludwig von Mises—is suspicious of 100 percent banking and considers it another example of government manipulation of private banking. The Chicago School sees 100 percent gold as too expensive, unable to achieve the ideal of a stable price level, and far too impractical. Finally, neo-Keynesian critics view the 100 percent proposal as too restrictive on the banking business, frequently inflationary, and unconductive to changes in the transitional demands of the public.

Most of these objections are refuted or denied by 100 percent advocates. They argue that the 100 percent banking plan is not just another restriction on the free market, but rather embodies the free market by enforcing contracts and eliminating fraud from the banking system. Nevertheless, it is worth noting that the ultra-hard money proponents are not entirely uncompromising: if, for example, 100 percent banking were not enforced as such, they would seem to favor "free banking" as the second best of "sound" monetary programs. As a "second best" solution, "free banking" would supposedly result in relatively high (though not 100 percent) reserves, depending on the competitive nature and redemption policies of banks. In order for "free banking" to work, however, banking would have to be "wholly free from all legislative interference," in the words of Sir Henry Parnell. Otherwise, "free banking" could be destabilizing, resulting in "wildcat banking." But according to Rothbard, "The horrors of 'wildcat banking' in America before the Civil War stemmed from two factors, both due to government rather than free banking: (1) Since the beginning of banking, in 1814 and then in every ensuing panic, state governments permitted banks to continue operating, making and calling loans, etc. without having to redeem in specie. In short, banks were privileged to operate without paying their obligations. (2) Prohibitions on interstate branch banking (which still exist), coupled with poor transportation, prevented banks from promptly calling on distant banks for redemption of notes."[120]

A pure metallic currency need not be "elastic," according to bullion-supporters, because prices are the only adjustment mechanism required to fulfill the needs of business and trade. Moreover, they deny that 100 percent banking would unduly restrain banking from offering useful services on an equitable basis. Equally, they deny instability of prices as a result of a gold inflation, arguing that much of the instability that occurred in the past during the gold discoveries was the result of national fractional reserve systems rather than a pure gold standard. In fact, Rothbard and Hayek appear to argue that a pure metallic standard lacks any cyclical characteristics which often beset fractional reserve systems.

The most difficult challenge facing the 100 percent specie plan is its alleged burden on society in terms of the high cost of labor and resources in the production of gold and silver. In response, hard money adherents do not necessarily view gold and silver extraction as a "waste of resources." Rather, the question becomes one of comparing the costs of one monetary standard with another, and determining which is the more expensive. Obviously, the cost of a pure paper money standard, unbacked by specie, is negligible from the point of view of expenses for printing government legal tender notes. However, according to Austrian economists, there are additional costs which override these great savings. This includes specifically the creation of a business cycle of inflation and depression on a successive basis, which can be tremendously expensive in terms of lost resources and labor. Rothbard maintains that this criticism equally applies to both fractional reserve systems (with either gold or Federal Reserve notes

---

120. Murray Rothbard, *Great Depression*, p. 309n.

as high-powered money) and a 100 percent fiat standard as proposed by the Chicago School and Irving Fisher. Any increase in a fiat money supply, transmitted through the loan markets, whether equal to annual productivity increases or not, still plants the seeds of misallocation of resources and cyclical patterns of boom and bust, followed by increased unemployment of labor and other factors of production.

Roger Garrison summarizes the "opportunity costs" of a paper money standard compared to a gold standard:

> The true costs of a paper standard would have to take into account (1) the costs imposed on society by different political factions in their attempts to gain control of the printing press, (2) the costs imposed by special-interest groups in their attempts to persuade the controller of the printing press to misuse its authority (print more money) for the benefit of special interests, (3) the costs in the form of inflation-induced misallocation of resources that occur throughout the economy as a result of the monetary authority succumbing to the political pressures of special interests, and (4) the costs incurred by businesses in their attempts to predict what the monetary authority will do in the future and to hedge against likely, but uncertain, consequences of monetary irresponsibility.[121]

Based on the above costs, Garrison concludes that "a gold standard costs less than a paper standard." He quotes a simile attributed to Alan Greenspan: "Allowing the state to create paper money is like putting a penny in the fuse box. The resource costs of the penny may be lower than the resource costs of the fuse, but the total costs, which take into account the likelihood of a destructive fire, are undoubtedly higher."[122]

---

121. Garrison, "The Costs of a Gold Standard," *The Gold Standard*, p. 69.
122. Ibid.

5

Conclusions

A number of important issues have been raised throughout this work and are worth examining at this point. These issues include the following: the origin of banking and the controversial role of the goldsmiths; the role of government in formulating a proper monetary framework (specifically, parallel standards vs. bimetallism, seigniorage, legal tender laws, and banking regulations); the question of "free banking," convertibility and redeemability; the question of elasticity of the currency, and stability of the price level under various "ideal" monetary standards; and finally, the paramount issue of paper money versus commodity money, and their strengths and weaknesses.

The Goldsmiths and the Origin of Banking

Clearly, the most significant development in the history of monetary systems in the Western world has been the introduction of tokens—tokens either in the form of coins or paper money, which occurred largely in the late Middle Ages and 17th century England. It was at this juncture that a monumental change took place in monetary history. Prior to this point in time, the Western world operated essentially on a 100 percent specie standard. However, with the introduction of paper money and cheap token coins, whose intrinsic value is far less than nominal or legal value, the ability of the fiscal authority to issue liabilities in excess of real money—coin and bullion—became readily apparent. What allowed this transformation to occur so rapidly was the result of two important factors: first, the homogeneous nature of money and money substitutes; and second, the inexpensive nature of token coins and paper money. These two factors established a tremendous incentive through the years to issue notes and obligations far in excess of assets held for redemption.

The legal ramifications of this excessive issue of bank and government obligations were a most perplexing problem facing the judicial system. The fungible nature of money was a legal stumbling block to the enforcement and preservation of a 100 percent monetary standard. Since the common law requirement for proof of theft or embezzlement of a client's funds was the identification of specific goods or funds which were stolen, fractional reserve banking was legalized by default, as it were. Unless *all* depositors demanded their money at once, which was certainly possible but highly improbable under normal circumstances, default and fraud could not be revealed and proven in the courts. It was a monumental victory for the bankers.

R. G. Hawtrey, Elgin Groseclose, Murray Rothbard, and others have frequently disparaged the character of the original goldsmiths who took advantage of the "law of great numbers" and lent out the demand deposits of their customers, who had left their valuables with them for safekeeping and did not mean to lend their money. According to their accusers, they were guilty of the fraudulent use of their customers' funds, in spite of legal sanctioning of the practice. Is this accusation justified? In considering the character of the goldsmiths, it is important to recognize their background. We note, for example, that prior to serving as repositors of investors' funds, the goldsmiths were experienced bullion dealers and were long accustomed to lending out their own funds to kings and other prominent citizens. When rich Englishmen withdrew their treasures from the poorly capitalized scriveners and the compromised Tower of London, and deposited their money for safekeeping with the goldsmiths, the use of these funds by the goldsmiths for lending purposes did not seem to be an unnatural or even an unlawful practice. For the scriveners, it might have been; for the goldsmiths, it did not seem so. It seems to have been almost a natural sequence to previous endeavors by the goldsmiths. And it was not long before the goldsmiths regarded these deposits as loans in return for the payment of a nominal interest paid on the balance.

Nevertheless, at the same time, the depositors did not really alter their view of demand deposits. They continued to see their deposits as still their own property and not as loans to the bank—a misconception that continues to this day. The blame for this misconception must be laid squarely on the original goldsmiths/bankers as well as the legal system which recognized the discrepancy but did not choose to incorporate this important distinction in banking law. Funds left by customers in the bank's vaults are still called "deposits" rather than "loans." Bankers and the courts have failed to come to grips with this widespread misconception, but have simply covered up the problem with federal deposit insurance, reserve requirements, and other banking regulations. Depositors, unfortunately, have seldom envisioned placing funds in banks as a form of *investment*, which it is in reality under the present banking structure, with relatively low or no rates of return, and relatively low levels of risk. Whether the legal framework of the banker/depositor relationship will ever coincide with the realities of the conceived notions of the public regarding the safekeeping of demand deposits is a matter of conjecture.

The Question of Bank Fraud

Supporters of the 100 percent rule insist that the modern banking practice of lending of customer's deposits is a legalized form of fraud. Deposits, notes and token coins are in reality warehouse receipts of property temporarily placed in storage. The use of these stored funds for bank profit is therefore a tort.

The central issue over the question of fraud seems to revolve around the homogeneity of money. Obviously, if money or money substitutes were *not* fungible in nature—i.e., not readily interchangeable—then virtually all legal authorities and economic analysts would readily agree that the unauthorized use of the customer's property would be fraudulent behavior. The case would be no different than a warehouse company renting out the furniture and other stored goods of its customers without their knowledge or consent. That is clearly illegal under present law regulating bailment.

But the point must be made that money is *not* like individual pieces of furniture or other stored items. Its very essence is homogeneity and fungibility. Otherwise is would cease to be money, and the medium of exchange. As Mises points out, money is neither a capital good nor a consumption good. It is never consumed, never the final object of our demands. Money stands alone as an intermediary, matching up the demand for and supply of a multitude of goods and services. Bearing this fact in mind, it appears that a strong case can be made that the use of money is far different from the use of other forms of property, and that the traditional lending of bank deposits can be conceived as a form of entrepreneurship rather than embezzlement. Fungibility is *sine qua non* to fractional reserve banking as well as money. On the other hand, fungibility does not require fractional reserves, but rather simply permits their existence. Thus, the homogeneity of money obscures the fraudulent nature of the fractional reserve banking system.

The Role of Government

Advocates of hard money and the 100 percent bullion standard have largely been suspicious of those in control of the monetary system, and in many cases have been first-hand witnesses to their harmful effects. They have been wary of such government policies as bimetallism, which sets an artificial rate of exchange between gold and silver in an attempt to establish a formal order in monetary affairs. But, contrary to the intentions of the fiscal authority, the measure has the opposite effect and leads to what has been called "Gresham's Law," where the undervalued currency is driven from circulation, while the overvalued coin is found in abundance. As an alternative, hard money supporters have opted for a free market approach of "parallel standards," where the rate of exchange between the two metals fluctuates according to market conditions.

Other examples where government interference of the monetary mechanism has been displayed and has been criticized, include legal tender laws, abolition of private coinage, use of national units of account such as dollars, francs, and pounds instead of weights of bullion, the excessive charges of seigniorage, and gratuitous coinage, which results in the gradual disappearance of domestically produced coins.

The Question of Free Banking: Stability, Convertibility, and Redeemability

There are essentially two isues confronting the question of "free banking." First, are demand deposits actually warehouse receipts for property temporarily placed under the custody of the banker, and redeemable on demand? Or are they really nothing more than promissory notes issued by the banker promising to convert a banknote or check into real money, or to transfer a specified amount of money from one account to another by check? Are banknotes redeemable or convertible? The dilemma here is similar to the one discussed in the preceding section. It appears that the depositor views demand deposits as warehouse receipts, while the banker and the government view them as promissory notes (interestingly enough, these two distinct views are the same with regard to *time* deposits). The "free banking" school conforms to this latter point of view. Perhaps there is a compromise to this dilemma. Why not allow bank customers the choice? They could be given the choice by a bank to accept banknotes or checks as either warehouse receipts, or as promissory notes, where the customer is made aware of the fact that this represents a loan to the bank, for which he receives little or no interest, but which could be withdrawn at any time by the customer. Under this solution, the legal framework would not compromise the beliefs of the public, and at the same time monetary freedom would be maintained.

Indeed, here is a major challenge to those "free market" economists who support the 100 percent specie standard. What fraud is committed if a customer voluntarily agrees to lend his banker his funds with the contractual agreement that the customer can withdraw his loaned funds on demand? This is surely a strong possibility under market conditions and is free from force or fraud. And yet, by permitting such contractual arrangements, a fractional reserve system is sure to develop on a broad scale.

The second issue raised here is that of market equilibrium of the private issuance of banknotes and other obligations. The free market school maintains that supply and demand work equally well in banking as they do in all other markets. Under competitive conditions, unhindered by legislative restrictions on branching, reserve requirements, and other aspects of the banking business, the school argues that supply and demand will result in an equilibrium level of reserves on the part of all banks—somewhere less than 100 percent, but probably higher than the present artificially low rates under the present Federal Reserve system. This equilibrium could be preserved under conditions of monetary order.

Surprisingly, the 100 percent adherents have granted their argument to a large degree, maintaining that "free banking," though containing some elements of fraud, would nevertheless provide a much "harder" and "sounder" system of banking than the present fractional reserve system. Thus, free banking becomes a "second best" solution that the ultra-hard money supporters would favor if the best of all monetary worlds were somehow rejected in the end. One important factor that Rothbard and others seem to have overlooked, however, is the destabilizing effects of a "slow credit expansion" that both schools of thought agree would occur under free banking. In other words, Mises, Rothbard and others admit that free banking would still permit a slow credit expansion to take place. How much depends on competitive market conditions. Rothbard suggests if only a few banks existed under "free banking," the inflationary process could last a long time.[1] Using the Hayek-Mises theory of the business cycle, these Austrians have pointed out that bank credit expansion necessarily leads to a boom-bust cycle, which in turn could easily disrupt the supposed stable nature of free banking, creating periods of speculation in high-risk investments on the part of the banks, resulting in re-

1. Rothbard, *The Mystery of Banking*, p. 119.

duced or negative earnings as the economy turns sour, and finally, undermining public confidence in banks during the depression stage of the cycle—and all this despite a presumption of high reserve levels. Thus, it appears that this "second best" solution may be nothing more than another bad solution to the monetary ills of the Western world, and it might be wise to reject the "free banking" solution on economic grounds alone, in spite of favorable philosophical implications.

Stability and the Price Level

Critics of the 100 percent specie proposal raise the issue of price stability and the inability of the commodity money to conform to changing economic conditions. In reply, the 100 percent defenders see their program as providing a stable foundation for the economy—at least far more stable than the present monetary system. Moreover, according to believers, any regional shifts in demand or resources will cause an adjustment to take place in prices, without any significant bottlenecks or lengthy periods of unemployment and depression. The issue of wage and price rigidity is usually dismissed or even ignored as a result of legislative bias favoring certain wage-earners and industries. Believers in the 100 percent commodity plan have little concern over the general price level, arguing that individuals in the marketplace are only concerned with specific prices, not an artificial general price index. There may be times when prices are generally rising or generally falling, but there should be no effort to maintain a level price index. This view, of course, is in sharp contrast with the Chicago School, which envisions a stable consumer price level through manipulations of a fiat money supply.

Paper Money Versus Commodity Money

A pure commodity standard has as its alleged chief drawback the high cost and financial burden to society. It costs literally billions of dollars every year to mine and process the precious metals. If the monetary demand for gold and silver were eliminated, most of the demand for specie would be solely for its industrial and artistic uses. Prices and profits in the metals would fall drastically (at least temporarily), allowing machinery, labor, and entrepreneur talent and management to move into other areas of economic endeavor related specifically to the production of goods and services of ultimate benefit to consumers.

As a side point, under the present monetary system of the international fiat dollar standard, the price of gold fluctuates far more than it would if gold were again central to all financial transactions and were the supreme numeraire of all countries' monetary systems. However, under a completely fiat system, with gold almost completely out of the system, the price of gold depends largely on the monetary policies of governments around the world. As Norman J. Silberling writes, "in an inconvertible system gold becomes a commodity, used chiefly in foreign payments along with bills; and that, far from being a fixed standard, to which all nations may 'unerringly refer,' it may become (especially under conditions such as exist at this juncture) an article subject to unusual fluctuations of demand and supply."[2] Of course, gold has yet to be relegated entirely to just "another commodity." It would take a completely stable monetary and economic environment for that to occur. But because of continued instability in the currency markets and monetary systems of the Western world, the price of gold is still affected by rates of inflation and world-shaking events. Gold has yet to become exogenous to the monetary system.

In choosing another "cheaper" monetary framework such as fiat paper money, there may well be greater costs of a different nature, as the Austrians state. A paper money standard, whether in the form of fractional reserves or a full Federal Reserve note standard, may prove to be counter-productive and cyclical in nature, creating an artificial expansion of credit followed by persistently high unemployment of labor and resources—all at a cost perhaps in excess of the savings that were supposed to be obtained by demonetization of the previous metals. There may be political costs as well, as Roger Garrison points out.

---

2. Norman J. Silberling, "Ricardo and the Bullion Report," in *Enterprise and Secular Change*, p. 380.

There are additional questions of interest. Would an annual expansion of the fiat money supply eventually lead to economic and monetary oscillations that would become greater and greater over time? Of equal importance, would a business cycle of the same proportions be created if the additional money supply were spent on consumption goods rather than investment goods through bank credit? These are questions that economists have not fully answered.

100 Percent Reserve Systems Today

It is interesting to note that, although the 100 percent specie standard has never been established in modern times on a national monetary scale, various forms of 100 percent banking have been in existence for many years. The most obvious, of course, is the safe deposit box available at most banks today.

There are some rather unusual examples too. Swiss banks have a long tradition of maintaining what they call "Custodial or Safekeeping Accounts," where the customer can have the bank purchase gold or silver bullion or foreign banknotes and have them stored for you. Under such legal arrangements, the gold is actually owned by the depositor and not the bank, so that if the bank failed, the gold could not be used to satisfy other creditors of the bank. Because gold bullion is homogeneous, the gold is stored physically with all the other customers' gold bullion, so that receipts are essentially "general warrant receipts," in the word of Jevons. Thus, this program amounts to a 100 percent specie system of banking, where the total number of gold ounces in the bank's vaults is equal to the total held by the customer on the bank's records, and bank auditors will periodically substantiate whether the physical holdings are equal to the total recorded on the bank's books. Also, it is illegal for the Swiss banks to use the gold for any purpose.

Custodial accounts are also offered by Swiss banks for storing currencies. In this case, the customer can ask for a "custodial account" in U.S. dollars, Swiss francs, German marks, or whatever currency the bank has available. The bank will then purchase actual banknotes in the currency you choose and will place them in an envelope. Your name, account number, and the amount of money you requested will be written on the envelope. The envelope will then be placed in the bank vault and left there—separate from all other currency banknotes—until further notice. If you want to withdraw some of the money, the bank will do so at your request and do with the currency as you wish. If the bank fails, the envelope of money is yours and is not an asset of the bank; nor can the bank use the banknotes to settle its debts.

The fees for these special "custodial accounts" are relatively inexpensive. The charges amount to 0.2 to 0.3 percent of the money involved. So on an account equivalent to $10,000, the annual charge would run about $20 to $30.

Unfortunately, these accounts do not operate as checking accounts, where you have the right of withdrawal by writing a check. You have to state in writing the purpose of the withdrawal and mail it to the bank, and then the bank will follow your instructions. However, several banks have recently offered "Specie Custodial Accounts" with the use of withdrawal by check on demand. Under this service, the depositor buys a specified amount of gold or silver bullion at the current spot price with U.S. dollars by sending a regular check to the bank. The bank then purchases the gold or silver bullion for the customer and stores it in the bank's vault. Special checks are then issued to the customer, allowing him the right to liquidate any portion of the bullion by writing a check in dollars. When the bank receives the check through the Federal Reserve clearing system, the bank liquidates the dollar value of the bullion according to the day's London fixing. The charges for this service are substantially higher than the "custodial accounts" offered by Swiss banks; the fee is one percent initially upon purchase and one percent of any amounts liquidated by check. Thus, if such an account were set up with $10,000, the charge would be $100 just to open the account. Such charges are, by the way, very comparable to those charged for outright purchases of bullion in the marketplace, although they are much higher than service fees on regular checking accounts.

This is not necessarily indicative of the charges that would prevail if banks were operating under a 100 percent specie standard.

The Issue of Practicality

One of the issues referred to from time to time with regard to the 100 percent specie standard is the question of practicality in being introduced at some time in the future. There are a number of astute criticisms that have been leveled at the 100 percent rule, and these concern the problems of bank evasion, disruptions of the economy due to the elimination of credit-induced distortion, and finally the ability for one nation to carry on such a radical program without the support of other nations.

Bank Evasion and Time Deposits

Several critics have pointed out how extremely able bankers have been in the past evading regulations such as the 100 percent rule. This occurred, for example after the enactment of the Peel Act of 1844 in England, which established a 100 percent reserve system for all future issues of notes and coins. Unfortunately, the Act did not include bank deposits under its regulations and consequently bankers were easily able to circumvent this regulation through bank deposits, which were not regarded as part of the money supply at the time. Thus, Hayek remarks, "It has been well remarked by the most critical among the originators of the scheme that banking is a pervasive phenomenon and the question is whether, when we prevent it from appearing in its traditional form, we will not just drive it into other and less easily controllable forms." After noting the historical precedent of the Act of 1844, Hayek predicts that "new forms of money substitutes would rapidly spring up."[3]

One present-day example of this problem exists with time deposits. In many cases, savings and loan associations and other banks offer "savings accounts" where you can withdraw your money on demand (or even by check in some areas of the country). The associations and banks retain the right to impose a 30-day time period before a customer can withdraw his money,

3. F. A. Hayek, *Monetary Nationalism*, pp. 82-83.

but this regulation is not enforced under normal circumstances.

Are these time deposits or demand deposits? According to Friedman, Rothbard, and others, they should be counted as demand deposits, subject to the 100 percent reserve requirement. But, then, how does the government deal with the bank that only insists on one day notice or one week notice? Are these deposits on time or on demand? If they are ruled to be time deposits, would this create a system of fractional reserves on a limited basis? To restrict banks from offering extremely short-term time deposits, perhaps the authorities could insist by law that all legitimate time deposits be required to last no shorter than the maturity of the bank loan. This requirement would be extremely inflexible and unsettling to the present money markets, however, since it would virtually wipe out any discounting of bonds and other loans.

Money market funds are a perplexing example in this regard. These funds are essentially liquid money market mutual funds that invest solely in high-yielding paper such as bank certificates of deposit, prime commercial paper, bankers' acceptances, and U.S. government securities such as 90-day and 180-day treasury bills. Since virtually all of these securities are marketable in the money markets at any time, the investors of these cash management funds are able to withdraw their money at any time by liquidating their shares, often through special checks. Here we have money market funds which appear in many ways as an example of 100 percent reserve banking, since for every dollar of securities purchased and invested, there is a dollar of securities stored for safekeeping. But more importantly, these funds reflect the dilemma facing advocates of the 100 percent reserve program. Here are legitimate *time* deposits which can be redeemed on demand. Is this another form of evasion of the 100 percent rule, and could it result in the artificial expansion of the money supply beyond reserves? This problem would be even more exacerbating with intermediate bond and municipal bond funds, where assets of the funds are long-term, but redemption is on demand with checking account privileges.

The Transition Period

The transition to a full 100 percent specie standard would be a difficult one and, according to critics, an intolerable one—involving huge increases in the price of gold and silver, massive shifts in international trade and the cash balances of individuals, and general disruption in the economy. According to Henry Hazlitt, an advocate of "free banking," "We could not return today to a 'pure' gold standard, of course, without an intolerable contraction of the money supply, but we could return to a system which locks the paper money and credit supply just where it is."[4]

Even Rothbard is aware of some of these almost insurmountable problems:

> Depending on how we define the money supply—and I would define it very broadly as all claims to dollars at fixed par value—a rise in the gold price sufficient to bring the gold stock to 100 per cent of total dollars would require a ten-to-twentyfold increase. This of course would bring an enormous windfall gain to the gold miners, but this does not concern us. I do not believe that we should refuse an offer of a mass entry into Heaven simply because the manufacturers of harps and angels' wings would enjoy a windfall gain. But certainly a matter for genuine concern would be the enormous impetus such a change would give for several years to the mining of gold, as well as the disruption it would cause in the pattern of international trade.[5]

Lessons From the Hard Money Tradition: A Restatement of Thesis

At the beginning of this paper, several outstanding economists were quoted on the waning influence of the hard money tradition on economic and monetary policy. Of special ironic note, both Hayek and Mises remarked how there is little if any *economic* sup-

---

4. Henry Hazlitt, "To Restore World Monetary Order," in Hans F. Sennholz, ed., *Gold Is Money* (Westport, Conn.: Greenwood Press, 1975), pp. 75-76.

5. Murray Rothbard, *The Case for 100 Percent*, pp. 39-40. See also his recent article, "The Case for a Genuine Gold Dollar," *The Gold Standard*, pp. 10-14.

port for a commodity or gold standard. And yet, using the very theories that they originated regarding the business cycle and credit, theoretical evidence is presented to show that a pure commodity standard, though perhaps costly in terms of resources (costs that may be unavoidable), does not exhibit the cyclical patterns of boom and bust that characterize a fiat money standard. If there is any lesson to be gained from this ironic note, it is that the leading supporters of the gold standard underestimate the power of their own theories and failed to see their full implications. The virtues of a pure fiat standard, even from an economic point of view, are simply not as pronounced, if we accept the conclusions of the Austrians. It raises the prospect that fiat money is not as "cheap" as it was thought previously.

In addition, the hard money partisans were instrumental over the past two or three centuries in providing lucid insights and criticism of the workings of a fractional reserve monetary system. Not only does this involve the legal and moral problems facing the banker/customer relationship, but it involves the harmful economic effects of international crises, excessive note issue, and inflationary recession. These are problems which are still unresolved today.

If there is to be one major thesis to be drawn from the history of economic thought regarding the 100 percent specie standard, it is that any international or domestic monetary standard founded partially or wholly on fiduciary elements will tend to be unstable and cyclical in nature. Relative instability and changes in the rate of production will depend on the quantity of fiat currency and the growth rate of the monetary base. According to this point of view, then, present monetary reform measures aimed at shifting away from a commodity or specie standard toward a fiduciary standard are likely to result in further economic disruption and eventually another international crisis.

In terms of political applications, the 100 percent supporters can probably do no more than play the role of the armchair critic. As this work has shown, the 100 percent specie standard, advantageous as it may be portrayed, can be instituted only through drastic reforms and economic disruptions. It may have theoretical beauty, but it lacks pedestrian attributes. Despite this pessimistic outlook, the 100 percent proponents have greatly contributed to economic science in: (1) developing a monetary program consistent with the free market; (2) emphasizing the central importance of bank deposits in determining the money supply and economic indicators; (3) detailing the harmful effects of bank credit expansion and central banking; (4) demonstrating the shortcomings of monetary systems which are established with less than a full-fledged commodity reserve, and (5) establishing the value of gold as a monitor of economic stability in the world.

Appendix

A Comparison of Four Monetary Standards

Throughout this work, four monetary standards have been referred to at some length. These systems are as follows: the 100 percent specie standard; the "free banking" system; the present fractional reserve system; and a 100 percent fiat money standard.

How does each of these monetary standards differ in terms of basic characteristics, the role of government, the determinants of the money supply, advantages and disadvantages (as seen by advocates and by critics), the practicality of introducing the plan, and the leaders of each monetary program? An outline of the differing characteristics and philosophies might assist us in the quest for an "ideal" monetary standard that will achieve stability and freedom, two important goals of the Western world.

The following divisions are made with regard to each monetary program.

Characteristics

100 Percent Specie Standard:

Monetary unit of account is either gold or silver. All demand deposits are warehouse receipts, requiring 100 percent reserves. Banker serves as a custodian or bailee of deposited funds and is forbidden to use them for personal profit under penalty of fraud. Banker may offer time deposits, but they cannot be withdrawn on demand, but may vary in length of maturity. Banker may also act as an intermediary between lenders and borrowers.

Parallel standards between prices of gold and silver.

Use of token coins as "representative money" for small change transactions.

Interest rates free to fluctuate according to supply and demand.

Free Banking:

Monetary unit of account is gold or silver. Banks are free to determine their own level of reserves, backed by specie. Time deposits are free to vary from demand deposits to long-term certificates. Government policy is strictly laissez faire, and not permitted to set reserve requirements, etc.

Parallel standards of price between gold and silver.

Use of token coins.

Fractional Reserve Banking:

Monetary unit of account: historically specie *or* banknotes issued by central bank. All demand deposits are loans to the bank and backed by specie or banknotes, depending on reserve requirements. Time deposits free to vary in maturity.

Reserves, set by the central bank, may only represent a small percentage of total deposits.

Use of token coins, not necessarily backed by any specie.

100 Percent Fiat Standard:

Monetary unit of account: Federal Reserve notes or banknotes issued by central bank. All demand deposits are warehouse receipts, requiring 100 percent reserves of banknotes or central bank deposits.

Time deposits cannot be withdrawn on demand but may vary in length of maturity.

Interest rates vary according to market conditions.

Use of token coins for small transactions, unbacked by specie.

Determinants of Money Supply

100 Percent Specie Standard:

Determined by supply and demand conditions of gold and silver, based on costs of production relative to other goods, and the demand for cash balances of the public.

Free Banking:

Determined by supply and demand for specie, and competitive banking conditions (the more rapid the redemption of banknotes, the higher the level of reserves, and thus the lower the bank multiplier in expanding bank credit).

Fractional Reserve Banking:

Determined by reserve requirements, open market operations by the central bank, and loan demand and interest rates charged to the public and institutions operating through banks.

100 Percent Fiat Standard:

Determined solely by the open market operations of the central bank.

Role of Government

100 Percent Specie Standard:

Primarily the role is in enforcement of 100 percent reserve requirement on demand deposits. Other roles might include coinage, enforcement of contracts, etc.

Free Banking:

Negligible role, complete laissez faire. Role restricted to coinage, minting, certification of weight and fineness of coins, etc. But strict laissez faire in granting charters, favors or laws on banking activities, reserve requirements, interstate branching, etc.

Fractional Reserve Banking:

Substantial government role. Establishment of reserve requirements by central bank, open market operations to influence interest rates and money supply, restrictions on branching and other banking activities, lending laws, deposit insurance, intervention in times of banking crisis, etc. Loan operations run by private banks under government supervision.

100 Percent Fiat Standard:

Government central and supreme in determining money supply. Interest rates and time deposits vary freely according to market conditions. Little role outside complete control of money supply and its growth, and enforcing 100 percent rule on demand deposits.

Advantages (As Seen by Advocates)

100 Percent Specie Standard:

Money virtually free from government manipulation. No discretionary power of government. Government limited to obtaining revenues through taxation or borrowing, not money-creation.

Provides legal rights of depositors, where ownership of funds remains in hands of depositors.

Elimination of monetary or government-induced inflation as well as business cycle, international crises, balance of payments deficits, Gresham's Law.

No monetary deflation, although prices may fall slowly.

Free Banking:

Monetary framework largely free from government control.

Provides a relatively hard money, sound banking system.

Provides a wide range of freedom in banking activities.

Fractional Reserve Banking:

Provides an "elastic" currency necessary to meet changes in seasonal and secular economic developments.

Provides numerous avenues for controlling the money supply and interest rates to meet social needs.

Provides direct control over monetary problems and unsound banking ventures. Relatively cheap monetary system with widespread use of paper money.

100 Percent Fiat Standard:

Ability to obtain goal of stable price level.

Makes monetary policy simple—central bank has full control of money supply at all times through simple device of open market operations.

Cheap money system with use of paper money and token coins.

Avoidance of wide variations in money supply growth.

Disadvantages (As Seen by Critics)

100 Percent Specie Standard:

Inability to let money supply fluctuate according to needs of business. Little or no elasticity.

Extremely expensive in terms of resources used in production of precious metals. Too restrictive on banking business. No allowance for government manipulation under "emergency" monetary crises.

Inability to provide a stable price level in the long run. Allows for periods of price deflation followed by high inflation during a "gold rush."

Free Banking:

Inability to eliminate entirely cyclical patterns in economy.

May be destabilizing because of business cycle and lack of ability of government to intervene in controlling reserve levels, which may end up too low because of lack of competition between banks.

Unsound banking practices and an excessive money supply could result in chaotic conditions.

Fractional Reserve Banking:

Difficulties in controlling the money supply in the short run, due to number of independent variables involved such as loan demand.

Legal relationship between depositor and banker is deceptive and hidden from public. Overdependence on each bank in maintaining stability of monetary system. One major failure seriously affects liabilities of related banks.

Gives too much power to central bank in controlling or increasing money supply, permitting excessive monetary inflation and subsequent recessions. International exchange crises and depression, balance of payments deficits.

100 Percent Fiat Standard:

Gives too much power to central bank allowing it to increase money supply too rapidly.

Creates cyclical patterns of boom and bust, with destabilizing effects on business and employment.

Practicality

100 Percent Specie Standard:

Highly impractical. It would mean substantial increase in price of gold and silver, resulting in great difficulties in foreign exchange markets and international trade.

May involve economic risks because of elimination of distortions created by monetary inflations in the past.

Great possibility of bank evasion methods.

Free Banking:

More practical than the 100 percent thesis. Central bank would buy and sell gold at free market prices, with all bank notes and deposits convertible at that price.

Substantial, radical change in bank branching; fluctuation in reserve requirements—the return of "wild-cat banking"?

Fractional Reserve Banking:

Present system. Characterized by unpredictable and unstable fluctuations in exchange rates, boom-bust business cycles, etc.

100 Percent Fiat Standard:

Fairly practical since present Federal Reserve notes are not backed by specie. Increasing reserves on demand deposists to 100 percent level would be a fairly easy bookkeeping task.

Radical change, however, on savings and loan associations and savings banks, which could no longer permit withdrawal of savings on demand.

Supporters

100 Percent Specie Standard:

Many hard money advocates including David Hume, the Currency School in England, Jacksonians and Jeffersonians in early 19th century, Charles Carroll, Amasa Walker, Elgin Groseclose, Murray Rothbard, Howard Katz, and others. Sympathetic support from Hayek and Friedman, among others.

Free Banking:

In certain degrees, the Banking School in England, Ludwig von Mises, Henry Hazlitt, Lysander Spooner, W. Stanley Jevons, William Brough, David Ricardo (in advocating convertibility), Lawrence White, George Selgin, and so on.

Fractional Reserve Banking:

Most bankers since the origin of banking, neo-Keynesian economists such as Paul A. Samuelson.

100 Percent Fiat Standard:

Irving Fisher, the Chicago School of Simons, Milton Friedman, et al.

Bibliography

Books

Adams, John. *Works*. Boston: Little, Brown & Co., 1856.

Adams, John Quincy. *Writings*. Edited by Worthington C. Ford. New York: Macmillan, 1916.

Amber, Charles H. *Thomas Ritchie, A Study in Virginia Politics*. Richmond: Bell Book and Stationery Co., 1913.

Beach, Frank Herman. *The Monetary Theories of John Law, An Abstract of a Thesis*. Urbana, Ill.: University of Illinois, 1933.

Böhm-Bawerk, Eugen von. *Capital and Interest*. South Holland, Ill.: Libertarian Press, 1959.

Bordo, Michael D. and Anna J. Schwartz, eds., *A Retrospective on the Classical Gold Standard*. Chicago: University of Chicago Press, 1984.

Brace, Harrison H. *Gold Production and Future Prices*. New York: Bankers Publishing Co., 1910.

Bronson, Henry. *The Money Problem*. 1877.

Brough, William. *The Natural Law of Money*. New York: Putnam, 1894.

_____________. *Open Mints and Free Banking*. New York: Putnam, 1898.

Burns, Arthur R. *Money and Monetary Policy in Early Times*. New York: Knopf, 1927.

Byrdsall, Fitzwilliam. *The History of the Loco-Foco or Equal Rights Party*. New York, 1842.

Cairnes, John E. *Essays in Political Economy*. New York: Augustus M. Kelley, [1873] 1965.

Carlile, W. W. *The Evolution of Modern Money.* London: Macmillian, 1901.

Carroll, Charles Holt. *Organization of Debt into Currency and Other Papers*. Edited by Edward C. Simmons. Princeton, N.J.: D. Van Nostrand Co., 1964.

Cernuschi, Henri. *Contre le billet de banque*. Paris, 1866.

Chase, Samuel P. *Legal Tender Cases*. 12 Wall 586.

Colwell, Stephen A. *The Ways and Means of Payment*. Second edition. 1860.

Conant, Charles A. *The Principles of Money and Banking*. New York: Harper, 1905. Two volumes.

Cox, James. *Metallic Money, Its Value and Its Function*. 1841.

Dolan, Edwin G., editor. *The Foundations of Modern Austrian Economics.* Kansas City: Sheed and Ward, 1976.

Dorfman, Joseph. *The Economic Mind in American Civilization*. New York: Viking Press, 1949.

Dunmar, Charles F. *The Theory and History of Banking*. New York: Putnam, 1901.

____________. *Chapters on the Theory and History of Banking*. New York: Putnam, 1907. Second edition.

Eichengreen, Barry editor. *The Gold Standard in Theory and History.* New York: Methuen, 1985.

Einaudi, Luigi. "The Theory of Imaginary Money from Charlemagne to the French Revolution." In Frederic C. Lane and Jelle C. Riemersma, eds., *Enterprise and Secular Change*. Homewood, Ill.: Irwin, 1953.

Elibank, Patrick Murray. *Essays*. 1755.

Farrand, Max, editor. *The Records of the Federal Convention of 1787*. New Haven, Conn., 1937.

Farrer, T. H. *Studies in Currency.* London: Macmillan, 1898.

Feaveryear, A. E. *The Pound Sterling*. Oxford: Clarendon Press, 1963.

Fisher, Irving. *The Instability of Gold*. New York: Alexander Hamilton Institute, 1912.

____________. *The Money Illusion*. New York: Adelphi Co., 1928.

____________. *100% Money*. New Haven, Conn.: The City Printing Co., 1945.

Friedman, Milton. *A Program for Monetary Stability*. New York: Fordham University Press, 1960.

Friedman, Milton and Anna J. Schwartz, *A Monetary History of the United States 1867-1960*. Princeton: Princeton University Press, 1963.

Gallatin, A. A. A. *Considerations, Etc*. 1831.

____________. *Writings*. Edited by Henry Adams. New York: 1960.

Geyer, Philip Joseph. *Banken und Krisen*. 1865.

Gouge, William M. *A Short History of Paper Money and Banking in the United States*. New York: B. & S. Collins, 1835.

Groseclose, Elgin. *Money, The Human Conflict*. Normal: University of Oklahoma Press, 1934.

____________. *Money and Man*. New York: Frederick Ungar, 1961.

Haberler, Gottfried. *Prosperity and Depression*. Geneva: League of Nations, 1939. Second edition.

Hansen, Alvin H. *Business Cycles and National Income*. New York: W. W. Horton, 1964.

Harris, Joseph. *An Essay Upon Money and Coins*. 1757-58.

Hawtrey, R. G. *The Gold Standard in Theory and Practice*. London: Longmans, Green and Co., 1933. Third edition.

____________. *Currency and Credit*. London: Longmans, Green and Co., 1937.

Hayek, F. A. *Prices and Production*. London: Routledge and Kegan Paul, 1935. Second edition.

____________. *Monetary Nationalism and International Stability*. New York: Longmans, Green and Co., 1937.

____________. *Individualism and Economic Order.* Chicago: University of Chicago Press, 1948.

____________. *The Denationalization of Money.* London: The Institute of Economic Affairs, 1976.

Hazlitt, Henry. *Return to Gold.* New York: Newsweek, 1954.

____________. *What You Should Know About Inflation.* New York: Funk and Wagnalls, 1965.

Horn, J. E. *La Liberte des Banques.* 1866.

Hume, David. *Political Discourses.* 1752.

Jacob, William. *An Historical Inquiry into the Production and Consumption of the Precious Metals.* New York: Augustus M. Kelley, [1831] 1968.

Jastram, Roy W. *The Golden Constant.* New York: John Wiley and Sons, 1977.

Jefferson, Thomas. *Writings.* Edited by T. E. Bergh. Washington, D.C.: Jefferson Memorial Association of the United States, 1904.

Jevons, W. Stanley. *Money and Mechanism of Exchange.* London: Kegan Paul, 1905. Fifteenth Edition.

Joplin, Thomas. *An Essay on General Principles and Present Practices of Banking.* London: Baldwin, 1826.

Katz, Howard. *The Paper Aristocracy.* New York: Books in Focus, 1976.

Kemmerer, E. W. *Gold and the Gold Standard.* New York: McGraw-Hill, 1944.

Kendall, Amos. *Autobiography.* Edited by William Stickney. Boston: P. Smith, 1872.

Keynes, John Maynard. *A Tract on Monetary Reform.* London: Macmillan, 1923.

____________. *Essays in Persuasion.* New York: Harcourt, Brace and Co., 1932.

____________. *The General Theory of Employment, Interest and Money.* New York: Harcourt, Brace and Co., 1936.

Lane, Frederic C. and Jelle C. Riemersma, eds. *Enterprise and Secular Change.* Homewood, Ill.: Irwin, 1953.

Laughlin, J. Laurence. *A New Exposition of Money, Credit and Prices*. Chicago: University of Chicago Press, 1931.

Law, John. *Considerations sur le numeraire et le commerce*. Edited by Daire. Paris, 1851.

Lee, Maurice W. *Macroeconomics: Fluctuations, Growth and Stability*. Homewood, Ill.: Richard D. Irwin, 1971.

Leggett, William. *A Collection of the Political Writings of William Leggett*. Edited by Theodore Sedgewick, Jr. New York, 1840.

Leroy-Beaulieu, Paul. *Traite d' Economie Politique*. Paris, 1910.

Loyd, Samuel Jones. *Reflections Suggested by a Perusal of Mr. J. Horsley Palmer's Pamphlet on the Causes and Consequences of the Pressure on the Money Market*. 1837.

Madison, James. *The Madison Papers*. Washington, D.C., 1840.

Martin, J. B. *Grasshopper in Lombard Street*. 1676.

Marx, Jenifer. *The Magic of Gold*. Garden City, N.Y.: Doubleday, 1978.

McCulloch, J. R. *Old and Scarce Tracts on Money*. London: King, 1933.

Menger, Carl. *Principles of Economics*. Edited by James Dingwall and Bert F. Hoselitz. Glencoe, Ill.: Free Press, 1950.

Miller, Harry E. *Banking Theories in the U.S. Before 1860*. Cambridge: Harvard University Press, 1927.

Mints, Lloyd W. *A History of Banking Theory*. Chicago: University of Chicago Press, 1945.

Mises, Ludwig von. *The Theory of Money and Credit*. New Haven: Yale University Press, 1953. Second edition.

____________. *Human Action*. Chicago: Henry Regnery Co., 1966. Third revised edition.

Niehans, Jurg. *The Theory of Money*. Baltimore: The Johns Hopkins University Press, 1978.

Nussbaum, Arthur. *Money in the Law, National and International*. Brooklyn, N.Y.: Foundation Press, 1950.

O'Connor, Michael J. L. *Origins of Academic Economics in the United States*. New York: Columbia University Press, 1944.

Paterson, Isabel. *The God of the Machine*. New York: G. P. Putnam's Sons, 1943.

Paul, Ron and Lewis Lehrman. *The Case for Gold*. Washington, D.C.: Cato Institute, 1982.

Pesek, Boris P. and Thomas R. Saving. *The Foundations of Money and Banking*. New York: Macmillan, 1968.

Pennsylvania Legislature. *Journal of the House*. 1820-21.

Phillips, C. A., T. F. McManus, and R. W. Nelson. *Banking and the Business Cycle*. New York: Macmillan, 1937.

Powell, E. T. *The Evolution of the Money Market*. London: Frank Cass and Co., 1966.

Raguet, Condy. *A Treatise on Currency and Banking*. Second edition. 1840.

Raymond, Daniel. *Thoughts on Political Economy*. Baltimore: F. Lucas, Jr. and E. J. Coale, 1820.

______________. *Elements of Political Economy*. Baltimore: F. Lucas, Jr. and E. J. Coale, 1823. Two volumes.

Read, Leonard. *Government—An Ideal Concept*. Irvington-on-Hudson, N.Y.: Foundation for Economic Education, 1954.

Ricardo, David. *Works of David Ricardo*. London: John Murray, 1876.

Richards, R. D. *The Early History of Banking in England*. London: Frank Cass & Co., 1958.

Ridgeway, William. *The Origin of Metallic Currency and Weight Standards*. Cambridge, Mass.: Wilson, 1892.

Robbins, Lionel. *Economic Planning and International Order*. London: Macmillan, 1937.

Robertson, Ross M. *History of the American Economy*. New York: Harcourt, Brace and World, 1964.

Rockwell, Llewellyn J., Jr., ed., *The Gold Standard: An Austrian Perspective*. Lexington, Massachusetts: Lexington Books, 1985.

Rogers, J. E. Thorold. *First Nine Years of the Bank of England*. London, 1887.

Röpke, Wilhelm. *Economics of a Free Society*. Chicago: Regnery, 1963.

Rothbard, Murray N. *Panic of 1819*. New York: Columbia University Press, 1962.

____________. *Man, Economy and State*. Los Angeles: Nash Publishing, 1970. Two volumes.

____________. *The Case for a 100 Percent Gold Dollar*. Washington, D.C.: Libertarian Press, 1974.

____________. *What Has Government Done to Our Money*. Santa Ana, Calif.: Rampart College, 1974.

____________. *America's Great Depression*. Kansas City: Sheed and Ward, 1975. Third edition.

____________. *The Mystery of Banking*. New York: Richardson and Snyder, 1983.

Samuelson, Paul A. *Economics*. New York: McGraw-Hill, 1970. Eighth edition.

Say, Jean-Baptiste. *A Treatise on Political Economy, or the Production Distribution and Consumption of Wealth*. Philadelphia: Claxton, Remsen and Haffelfinger, 1880.

Schumpeter, Joseph A. *History of Economic Analysis*. New York: Oxford University Press, 1954.

Schwartz, Anna J. *Money in Historical Perspective*. Chicago: University of Chicago Press, 1987.

Selgin, George A. *The Theory of Free Banking*. Totowa, N.J.: Rowman & Littlefield, 1988.

Sennholz, Hans F., editor. *Gold is Money*. Westport, Conn.: Greenwood Press, 1975.

____________. *Inflation or Gold Standard?* Lansing, Mi.: Constitutional Alliance, 1975.

Siegel, Barry N., ed. *Money in Crisis*. San Francisco: The Pacific Institute for Public Policy Research, 1984.

Simons, Henry C. *A Positive Program for Laissez Faire*. Chicago: University of Chicago Press, 1934.

———. *Economic Policy for a Free Society.* Chicago: University of Chicago Press, 1948.

Sklar, Robert O. and Benjamin W. Palmer. *Business Law.* New York: McGraw-Hill, 1942.

Slade, William. *Banks or No Bank.* N.d.

Smart, William. *Economic Annals of the Nineteenth Century.* New York: Augustus M. Kelley, 1964. Two volumes.

Smith, Adam. *An Inquiry into the Nature and Causes of the Wealth of Nations.* New York: The Modern Library, [1776] 1937.

Smith, Vera C. *The Rationale for Central Banking.* London: King, 1936.

Spahr, Walter E. and James Washington Bell, editors. *A Proper Monetary and Banking System for the United States.* New York: Ronald Press, 1960.

Spencer, Herbert. *Social Statics.* New York: Robert Schalkenbach Foundation, 1954.

Spooner, Lysander. *A Letter to Grover Cleveland.* Boston: Tucker, 1886.

Stamp, Sir Josiah. *Papers on Gold and the Price Level.* London: P. S. King & Sons, 1931.

Sylvester, Isaiah W. *Bullion Certificates as Currency.* New York: U.S. Assay Office, 1882.

Tracy, Antoine Destutt de. *Treatise on Political Economy.* Georgetown, Washington, D.C., 1817.

Vethake, Henry. *The Principles of Political Economy.* 1838.

Virginia General Assembly. *Journal of the House of Delegates*, 1820-21.

Walker, Amasa. *Nature and Uses of Money and Mixed Currency, with A History of the Wickaboag Bank.* Boston: Crosly, Nichols, and Co., 1857.

———. *The Science of Wealth.* Boston: Little, Brown, 1874. Third edition.

Walker, Francis A. *Political Economy.* New York: Henry Holt and Co., 1888.

______________. *Money in its Relations to Trade and Industry.* New York: Henry Holt and Co., 1889.

______________. *Money.* New York: Holt, 1891.

White, Lawrence H. *Free Banking in Britain, 1800-1845*. Cambridge: Cambridge University Press, 1984.

Wicksell, Knut. *Lectures on Political Economy.* New York: Macmillan, 1935.

Wilson, James, Esq. *Capital, Currency, and Banking*. London: D. M. Hird, 1859.

Wu, Chi-Yuen. *An Outline of International Price Theories*. London: Routledge, 1939.

Yeager, Leland B., editor. *In Search of a Monetary Constitution.* Cambridge: Harvard University Press, 1962.

Pamphlets

Hume, David. "Banks and Paper Money." Financial Pamphlet, vol. 22.

Parnell, Sir Henry. "Observations on Paper Money, Banking and Overtrading, including those parts of the evidence taken before the Committee of the House of Commons which explained the Scotch System of Banking." Pamphlet. 1827.

Dissertations

Yeager, Leland B. "An Evaluation of Freely-Fluctuating Exchange Rates." Unpublished Ph.D. dissertation, Columbia University, 1952.

Articles

Angell, James W. "The 100 Per Cent Reserve Plan," *Quarterly Journal of Economics*, 50:34 (November, 1935).

Bradford, Gamaliel. "Lombard and Wall Street," *North American Review*, XIX, 1874.

______________. "Three Systems of Currency," in *Transactions of the National Association for the Promotion of Social Science*. 1875.

Carroll, Charles Holt. "The Currency and the Tariff." *Hunt's Merchants' Magazine and Commercial Review*, XXXIII (August 1855), pp. 191-199.

Friedman, Milton. "Real and Pseudo Gold Standards," *Journal of Law and Economics* 4 (October, 1961), pp. 66-79.

Friedman, Milton and Anna J. Schwartz. "Has Government Any Role in Money?" *Journal of Monetary Economics* (January, 1986), pp. 37-62.

Hart, Albert G. "The 'Chicago Plan' of Banking Reform," *Review of Economic Studies*, 2:104-116 (1935).

Garrison, Roger W., "Gold: A Standard and an Institution," *Cato Journal* 3:1 (Spring, 1983), pp. 233-238.

Graham, Frank D. "Partial Reserve Money and the 100 Per Cent Proposal," *American Economic Review*, XXVI (1936), pp. 428-40.

Longfield, Mountifort. "Banking and Currency," *Dublin University Magazine*, February 1840.

Magee, J. D. "The World's Production of Gold and Silver from 1493 to 1905," *Journal of Political Economy* (May, 1909).

Reynolds, Alan. "Why Gold?" *Cato Journal* 3:1, 1983, pp 211-232.

Rothbard, Murray. "The Myth of Free Banking in Scotland," *The Review of Austrian Economics* 2 (1987), pp. 229-245.

Salerno, Joseph T. "Gold Standards: True and False." *Cato Journal*, 3:1, 1983, pp. 239-267.

Trimble, William. "Diverging Tendencies in New York Democracy in the Period of the Locofocos," *American Historical Review*, #3, April 1919.

Tucker, Refus S. "Gold and the General Price Level," *Review of Economic Statistics* (July, 1934).

Name Index

Subject Index

About the Author

Mark Skousen is an international economist and financial author. In 1977, he received his Ph.D. in economics from George Washington University, where he specialized in money and banking.

Since 1980, Mr. Skousen has served as editor of a monthly financial newsletter, *Forecasts & Strategies*, published by Phillips Publishing Inc. in Potomac, Maryland. He is the author of 16 books, including *The Structure of Production* (New York University Press, 1990), *Economics on Trial* (Irwin, 1991), *Dissent on Keynes* (Praeger, 1992), and *Puzzles and Paradoxes in Economics* (Edward Elgar, 1996), co-authored with Ken Taylor. His financial books include *The Complete Guide to Financial Privacy* (Simon & Schuster, 1982), *The Investor's Bible: Mark Skousen's Principles of Investment* (Phillips Publishing, 1992), and *Scrooge Investing* (Little, Brown, 1995).

Prior to entering the investment advisory business, Mr. Skousen was an economist for the Central Intelligence Agency from 1972 to 1974.

Currently, Mr. Skousen is Adjunct Professor of Economics and Finance at Rollins College, Winter Park, Florida 32789. He writes a monthly column for *The Freeman*, published by the Foundation for Economic Education, and is an occasional contributor to *Forbes*, *Reason*, *Human Events*, and *Liberty* magazine.

About the Publisher

The Foundation for Economic Education, Inc., was established in 1946 by Leonard E. Read to study and advance the moral and intellectual rationale for a free society.

The Foundation publishes *The Freeman,* an award-winning monthly journal of ideas in the fields of economics, history, and moral philosophy. FEE also publishes books, conducts seminars, and sponsors a network of discussion clubs to improve understanding of the principles of a free and prosperous society.

FEE is a non-political, non-profit 501(c)(3) tax-exempt organization, supported solely by private contributions and sales of its literature.

For further information, please contact: The Foundation for Economic Education, Inc., 30 South Broadway, Irvington-on-Hudson, New York 10533. Telephone (914) 591-7230; fax (914) 591-8910.